1000 Breaking Bad Facts

Scott Ambrose

CONTENTS

INTRODUCTION

Breaking Bad is a critically acclaimed television series that captivated audiences with its gripping storyline and complex characters. Created by Vince Gilligan, the show follows the transformation of high school chemistry teacher Walter White into a ruthless drug kingpin. Set in Albuquerque, New Mexico, Breaking Bad explores themes of morality, power, and the consequences of one's actions.

This fact book delves into the world of Breaking Bad, providing readers with fascinating insights about the making of the show, behind-the-scenes trivia, and details about the unforgettable characters that made it a cultural phenomenon. Join us as we journey into the world of Breaking Bad and uncover the secrets behind this groundbreaking series.

1000 BREAKING BAD FACTS

(1) Mike Ehrmantraut is a United States Marine Corps veteran - which would explain why he's a handy person to have on your side and a dangerous person to have as an enemy.

(2) The bell used by the wheelchair bound Hector Salamanca in Breaking Bad sold for $26,750 at an auction in 2013.

(3) Madrigal executive Lydia is very fond of chamomile tea and takes it with soy milk and artificial sweetener. This could be considered unconventional because chamomile tea doesn't really need anything to be added to it. Chamomile tea gives us an insight into Lydia's character because it is a mild relaxant and sedative. If you are wondering why Lydia puts milk in her chamomile tea it is because Breaking Bad creator Vince Gilligan also does this - which he admits is a strange thing to do.

(4) After the death of Gale Boetticher, Hank is much amused by a DVD found in Gale's apartment of Gale performing karaoke - though Walter White is (for understandable reasons) obviously not amused at all when he views it. The song that Gale is performing is the sci-fi themed Major Tom (Coming Home) by Peter Schilling from his album Error in the System. This song was released in 1983 and a huge hit in Europe - well, apart from Britain (where it stalled at 42 in the charts). Peter Schilling is a German synthpop musician. There are Thai subtitles on Gale's performance - which obviously means he was on vacation abroad at the time.

(5) The 1983 gangster film Scarface, which we see Walt and Walt Jr watching in Breaking Bad, featured two Breaking Bad actors - Steven Bauer (who played Don Eladio Vuente in Breaking Bad) and Mark Margolis (who played Hector Salamanca in Breaking Bad). There is another connection too as Míriam Colón, who played Tony Montana's mother in Scarface, also played Abuelita Salamanca in Better Call Saul.

(6) A pink teddy bear is used as a motif in Breaking Bad. The teddy ends up in Walter's pool after the plane crash caused by the grief stricken air traffic controller Donald Margolis - which Walter White had a hand in himself given that he watched Donald's daughter die. The pink teddy bear represents Walter's guilt and all the damage he has done.

(7) The pink of the fallen teddy bear in the b/w scenes in Breaking Bad is inspired by the little girl with the red coat in Schindler's List.

(8) Mike Ehrmantraut is clearly a fan of old movies because he's often watching them when we see him at home in Breaking Bad and Better Call Saul. Among the films we see him watching are The Big Heat, The Caine Mutiny, His Girl Friday, The Mouse That Roared, and The Awful Truth. The films we see Mike watching are ones owned by Sony - the parent company behind Breaking Bad. By using Sony owned films they obviously didn't have to pay anyone to get the rights for these clips.

(9) ABC, NBC, Showtime, TNT, FX and HBO were among the networks who rejected Breaking Bad.

(10) Jesse's full name is Jesse Bruce Pinkman.

(11) Mike's beloved granddaughter Kaylee Ehrmantraut is portrayed by Kaija Roze Bales in Breaking Bad. Three different child actors then portrayed the character in Better Call Saul. As some fans noted, the two shows are a trifle inconsistent when it comes to Kaylee's age. She is said to be ten in season five of Breaking Bad but in Better Call Saul - which is supposed to be several years earlier - still looks about the same age as she did in Breaking Bad.

(12) Gus Fring poisons Don Eladio Vuente via the vintage tequila he brought as a gift. The brand of tequila is Zafiro Añejo. This is a fictional brand they made up for the show. Real life brands were unsurprisingly not too keen on having their product poison someone in a television show! Zafiro Añejo also features in Better Call Saul. Jimmy buys a bottle of Zafiro Añejo in one scene - which costs him $495.

(13) In preparation for playing Walter White, Bryan Cranston sat in on some classes at a real high school so that he could observe teachers at work.

(14) Marie compares Walter to Ted Kaczynski in the last ever episode. Ted Kaczynski, also known as the Unabomber, is an American domestic terrorist and former mathematician who carried out a nationwide bombing campaign from 1978 to 1995. He targeted individuals involved in modern technology and aviation, killing three people and injuring 23 others. Kaczynski was eventually arrested in 1996 and sentenced to life in prison without the possibility of parole

(15) In the season five episode Granite State, we see that the New Hampshire cabin Walter is hiding out in only has two DVDs on the shelves - both of which are Mr Magorium's Wonder Emporium. This is a 2007 fantasy

film which got terrible reviews. No wonder Walt has cabin fever!

(16) It is sometimes reported that John Cusack turned down the part of Walter White but this is not true. Cusack, in response to a question about this, said on social media that he was never offered the part.

(17) Vince Gilligan more or less likened the arc of Walter White to a supervillain origin story. Walter is a sympathetic character at the start of Breaking Bad and we root for him. However, as we go deeper into the show we see that Walter is not really a very nice person and are increasingly forced to question our feelings towards him.

(18) Walter uses Lily of the Valley to poison Brock. The Lily of the Valley plant (Convallaria majalis) contains toxic substances called cardiac glycosides, which can be harmful if ingested in large quantities. Eating any part of the plant, including the leaves, flowers, or berries, can cause symptoms such as vomiting, diarrhea, dizziness, and a slowed heart rate.

(19) The season three episode Fly is what is known as a bottle episode and revolves around Walter and Jesse in the lab, making meth, talking, and trying to catch a pesky fly. A bottle episode is a term used in television to describe an episode that takes place primarily in one location, typically due to budget constraints. The term originated from the idea of a ship in a bottle, where all the characters are trapped in a confined space for the duration of the episode. Fly was a consequence of the show going over budget and having to do an episode that wouldn't cost much money. You could probably describe Fly as one of the more divisive episodes of Breaking Bad but most people seem to like it.

(20) Ozymandias is a sonnet written by the English poet Percy Bysshe Shelley and was first published in 1818. The poem was inspired by the discovery of a statue of the Egyptian pharaoh Ramesses II (also known as Ozymandias) in the ruins of the ancient city of Thebes. The poem explores themes of power, pride, and the inevitable decay of all things. It tells the story of a traveler who encounters a ruined statue in the desert, which serves as a reminder of the fleeting nature of human achievements. The inscription on the statue reads, "My name is Ozymandias, king of kings: Look on my works, ye Mighty, and despair!" Despite the grandiose claims of the statue, all that remains of Ozymandias' empire is a fallen statue in the desert, surrounded by vast and empty sands. The poem serves as a stark reminder of the transitory nature of power. Ozymandias is also the superhero name of Adrian Veidt - a pivotal character in the classic Alan Moore comic book series Watchmen.

(21) A few years before Breaking Bad there was a Showtime drama called Weeds which had a similar sort of premise. The show was about a widowed mother named Nancy Price Botwin (Mary-Louise Parker) who begins selling marijuana to support her family. As the show goes on, Nancy gets deeper and moves higher up in the drugs racket. Vince Gilligan said that if he'd been aware of Weeds he probably wouldn't have written Breaking Bad for fear that he was copying that show.

(22) Gus Fring's name was inspired by the German footballer Torsten Frings.

(23) The character Mike Ehrmantraut was written into Breaking Bad as a sort of substitute for Saul Goodman when Bob Odenkirk had a schedule conflict. Bob Odenkirk obviously returned to Breaking Bad when his

schedule was clear again and - happily - Mike Ehrmantraut stuck around too. The scene they created Mike for was where he cleans up the apartment and tells Jesse what to do after Jane's death. Saul was originally going to be the character who did this.

(24) Gus Fring has fourteen branches of Los Pollos Hermanos restaurants. The business, though profitable, is used as a disguise by Fring so that he can pose as a respectable businessman and pillar of the community. In reality he uses Los Pollos Hermanos trucks to smuggle drugs. His poultry farm on the outskirts of Albuquerque serves as a secret distribution/business headquarters.

(25) It is implied that Gus Fring was connected to Pinochet's regime in Chile. Augusto Pinochet was a military general and dictator who ruled Chile from 1973 to 1990. He came to power in a military coup that overthrew the democratically elected socialist government of Salvador Allende. Pinochet's regime was marked by widespread human rights abuses, including political repression, torture, and killings of political opponents. He implemented economic policies that greatly benefited the wealthy elite but led to social inequality and poverty for many Chileans.

(26) Methamphetamine is a powerful and highly addictive central nervous system stimulant that is commonly abused for its euphoric effects. It can be smoked, snorted, injected, or swallowed, and is known by various street names such as meth, crystal, ice, and crank. Meth has been called the 'poor man's cocaine' due to the fact it is more affordable.

(27) Although you see Walter and Jesse make a lot of meth in Breaking Bad you never see the whole process or

get the whole process explained to you. The writers on the show were advised by the DEA on meth production but the DEA didn't tell them the whole process. The people making the show and the DEA obviously didn't want to teach people watching at home how to make methamphetamine!

(28) Walter White and his team rob a train to steal methylamine in Breaking Bad. Some science buffs have suggested this could be seen as a bit of a goof because a clever man and chemistry expert like Walter White should know how to synthesize methylamine (and thus make robbing a train unnecessary).

(29) Jesse Pinkman is a big fan of Funyuns. Funyuns are a popular snack food that consists of onion-flavored rings made from cornmeal and seasoned with various spices.

(30) The top rated episode of Breaking Bad on IMDB is Ozymandias with a perfect 10/10.

(31) The second highest rated episode of Breaking Bad on IMDB is Felina with a score of 9.9

(32) A Colombian remake of Breaking Bad called Metástasis ran in 2014. It followed the original closely and was basically a remake in Spanish - only on a much lower budget. Metástasis got terrible reviews on IMDB and is more of a curiosity than anything. Bryan Cranston did praise the show though for being inventive with its modest budget. Walter is called Walter Blanco in the show. The Jesse Pinkman character is called José Miguel Rosas.

(33) Walter is given a new identity by Ed Galbraith when he has to go into hiding. His new surname is Lambert.

This is the maiden name of his wife Skyler.

(34) Giancarlo Esposito was born in Denmark to an Italian father and African-American mother. He moved to the United States when he was six. This is why native speakers of Spanish say you can tell that Gus Fring's Spanish isn't natural. Giancarlo Esposito obviously isn't a native Spanish speaker.

(35) If you want a new identity from the vacuum cleaner repairman Ed Galbraith you have to call his shop and ask for a dust filter for a Hoover Max Extract Pressure Pro, Model 60. This product doesn't need a dust filter because it is a carpet cleaner. No one would actually ask for this - unless they wanted Galbraith's 'real' services.

(36) Vince Gilligan got his break writing for The X-Files. It was actually an appearance in The X-Files by Bryan Cranston that gave Gilligan the idea of casting him as Walter White.

(37) Gus Fring constructs a high tech 'superlab' under a laundry business as a place where Walter White can produce methamphetamine of a high quality and on a large scale. The idea of a secret methamphetamine superlab is not fiction but something which comes from real life true crime. The Sinaloa Cartel were one of a number of criminal gangs who constructed superlabs to produce drugs on an industrial scale. The Sinaloa Cartel is one of the most powerful and notorious drug trafficking organizations in Mexico. It was founded in the 1980s by Joaquín "El Chapo" Guzmán, who became one of the most famous and powerful drug lords in Mexico. The cartel is known for its involvement in the production, trafficking, and distribution of drugs such as cocaine, marijuana, and methamphetamine. It has operations in

several countries, including the United States, and has been responsible for a significant amount of violence and corruption in Mexico. Superlabs tend to operate outside of the United States for obvious reasons. The chemicals used to make meth are more tightly controlled in the United States than Mexico. In reality these superlabs would be larger than the one Gus has in Breaking Bad and not as pristine.

(38) Jesse says the word 'bitch' 54 times in Breaking Bad.

(39) One of the things that makes Mike Ehrmantraut so good at his job as an enforcer/right-hand man for Gus Fring and 'clean up' operator/spy for Saul Goodman is that Mike used to be a cop in Philadelphia. His years in the police have given him extensive knowledge on the way law enforcement works and also how criminals think and operate.

(40) Walt's secret is revealed in Breaking Bad when Hank finds the Walt Whitman book Leaves of Grass that Gale gifted Walt. Walt Whitman was an American poet, essayist, and journalist who is often considered one of the most influential and innovative poets in American literature. Whitman was born in 1819 in Long Island, New York. Gale Boetticher is very taken with the poem When I Heard the Learn'd Astronomer. When I Heard the Learn'd Astronomer reflects on the limitations of scientific knowledge and the beauty of nature. The speaker describes sitting in a lecture hall listening to a knowledgeable astronomer speak about the stars and planets, but feeling disconnected and removed from the wonder of the natural world. Instead of finding fulfillment in the academic discourse, the speaker yearns to go outside and experience the beauty of the universe firsthand.

(41) There was actually a fan theory early on that Steve Gomez was a DEA plant and was really working for Gus Fring. This obviously didn't turn out to be true though.

(42) Giancarlo Esposito said his yoga classes helped him to develop the very calm and controlled persona of Gus Fring.

(43) The museum that Jesse and Jane go to is celebrating the work of Georgia O'Keeffe. Georgia O'Keeffe was an American modernist artist known for her large-scale paintings of flowers, landscapes, and other natural forms. She was one of the most influential and innovative female artists of the 20th century, and was a pioneer of American modernism.

(44) SaveWalterWhite.com., the website that Walt Jr sets up to fundraise for his dad, is actually online and a page you can visit. If you click on the donate page you are simply taken to the AMC website. You obviously can't really donate money!

(45) There was going to be a plot in season three where Walter tries to persuade an incarcerated South American drug baron to help him take down Gus Fring. In the end they decided not to do this plot because there simply wasn't room for it.

(46) Jesse is a fan of the Grand Slam breakfast. The Grand Slam breakfast is a popular menu item at Denny's restaurants. It typically includes two eggs, bacon strips, sausage links, hash browns, and pancakes or toast.

(47) Walter and Jesse had to dispose of a victim in acid early in the show. This is something that cartels and some killers do in real life. Jesse makes a mistake when he puts

hydrofluoric acid in the bath rather than a plastic container. The TV show Mythbusters said the sequence where Jesse's bath melts and falls through the ceiling is not accurate because hydrofluoric acid would not melt through a bath like that.

(48) 4 Days Out was supposed to be a money saving bottle episode which took place almost entirely in the RV. In the end though a lot of outdoor shooting took place - making the episode considerably more expensive than planned.

(49) Walter White prides himself on making a very pure version of meth. This is what makes him successful when it comes to crime - the drug he produces is better than the competition. Some crime journalists have suggested this business model would not really work in reality because desperate meth addicts would probably not notice or even care. It's not like comparing a fine wine!

(50) DEA stands for Drug Enforcement Administration. The Drug Enforcement Administration is a United States law enforcement agency responsible for combating the illegal drug trade and enforcing federal drug laws. The DEA investigates drug trafficking organizations, enforces drug laws, and works to disrupt the flow of illegal drugs into the country.

(51) Aaron Paul named 4 Days Out as his favorite episode. This is the episode where Jesse and Walt have RV trouble and get stranded in the desert.

(52) Mike's surname Ehrmantraut was only made known in episode 11 of Season 4.

(53) The real shooting location for Walter White's house

was 3828 Piermont Drive in Albuquerque. This is a real house. The owners of the house got so fed up with Breaking Bad tourists in the end that they put a steel fence around the front. Apparently, some fans even tried to recreate the scene in Caballo Sin Nombre where an angry Walt throws a pizza and it lands on the roof.

(54) Bryan Cranston was not told by the writers that Walter had poisoned Brock before he played the scene where Walter denies doing this to Jesse. This made Walter seem very convincing during the scene - which was the whole point. Walter has grown into a very accomplished liar.

(55) Gray Matter Technologies was the company that Walter White founded with his college classmate Elliott Schwartz. Schwartz means black in German - which blended with White makes Gray. Walter was engaged to his lab assistant Gretchen at the company. However, Walter backed out of the relationship because he was intimidated by Gretchen coming from a wealthy family. He sold his share in the company for $5,000 and ended up as a high school chemistry teacher. Gretchen married Elliot Schwartz and Gray Matter Technologies became a highly successful company worth a couple of billion. Walter's shares would have been worth millions in the end if he hadn't sold them. Walter White plainly regrets this decision as it would have given his family financial security for life - even if he wasn't around.

In the spin-off show Better Call Saul, Walter cites selling those shares as his biggest regret. When he is exposed as Heisenberg and a wanted man, Walter is enraged when he sees Elliot and Gretchen on television downplaying his role in the company and saying he did nothing except come up with the name. Elliot and Gretchen are plainly distancing themselves from Walter for company PR and feel safe to say whatever they want about him now. That rather backfires because Walter pays them a visit and uses them as a means to get his money to Walt Jr.

(56) Robert Forster, who played Ed Galbraith (the vacuum salesman/repairman who can give you a new life and identity), was actually a vacuum cleaner salesman in real life at one point.

(57) Jesse is very impressed by the green beans with almonds when he has dinner with Walter and Skyler. Turns out though that Skylar got them from the deli. If you want to make this recipe all you have to do is add lemon, garlic, and season with salt and pepper.

(58) Vince Gillgan said that one of the endings they considered for Breaking Bad was having Walt, Skylar, and Walt Jr all given a new identity by Ed Galbraith and leave town together. The reason why they decided not to do this ending is that they didn't think it was credible that Walt Jr would have agreed to do this.

(59) Saul Goodman tells (an unimpressed) Walter White that he can be his Tom Hagen in Breaking Bad. Tom Hagen was the consigliere and lawyer for the Corleone family in the first two classic Godfather films.

(60) The character Ted Beneke breaks his neck in Breaking Bad. The ironic thing about this is that Christoper Cousins, who played Ted, had just had spinal surgery in real life.

(61) Bryan Cranston came up with Walter's look at the start of the show - his hairstyle, moustache, and slight paunch. He wanted Walter to feel like a weary, mundane,

and average man so that his transformation into Heisenberg would be more effective. It was also Cranston's idea for Heisenberg to wear a hat.

(62) Jonathan Banks had a long and eclectic career before Breaking Bad. He was in films like Beverly Hills Cop and 48 Hrs. On television he was in everything from Hill Street Blues to Diagnosis: Murder to Star Trek: Deep Space Nine. The specific thing that got him cast in Breaking Bad was apparently his role in Wiseguy. Wiseguy is an American crime drama television series that aired on CBS from 1987 to 1990. The show follows undercover operative Vinnie Terranova as he infiltrates various criminal organizations to gather intelligence for his bosses at the Organized Crime Bureau. Created by Stephen J. Cannell, Wiseguy was praised for its complex storytelling, well-developed characters, and gritty realism. Banks played senior FBI agent Frank McPike in 74 episodes of Wiseguy.

(63) Vince Gillgan said that the darkest ending to Breaking Bad would have been for everyone to die - all except for Walter White!

(64) The fast food chain Los Pollos Hermanos owned by Gustavo Fring is fictional but - in tribute to the show - some Los Pollos Hermanos pop-up restaurants have been opened. A branch of Twisters in Albuquerque was used for the scenes involving Los Pollos Hermanos. Twisters is a real restaurant chain which serves Mexican cuisine.

(65) Julia Minesci played the rather haggard and world weary meth addicted hooker Wendy in the first two seasons of Breaking Bad. In real life Julia is actually a fitness fanatic who runs marathons.

(66) We see Walter eating cereal several times in the show. Raisin Bran cereal and Cheerios seem to be his favorites.

(67) Walter White Jr suffers from cerebral palsy. Cerebral palsy is a group of neurological disorders that affect movement, muscle tone, and coordination. It is caused by abnormal development or damage to the parts of the brain that control movement and balance. Symptoms can vary from mild to severe and may include muscle stiffness, weakness, tremors, and difficulty with coordination and balance. RJ Mitte, the actor who played Walter White Jr, also suffers from cerebral palsy but a milder form than the character he played in Breaking Bad. Mitte said he did some extra research on cerebral palsy when he played Walter White Jr to make his performance more realistic.

(68) Vince Gilligan said it took nineteen takes to get the shot of Gus Fring emerging from Hector's room after the explosion.

(69) Breaking Bad was originally going to be set in Riverside, California. The decision to set the show in New Mexico was a consequence of a 25% tax rebate on offer for locating the show there. The fact that New Mexico is fairly close to the border obviously added fresh possibilities to the story.

(70) One of the things that appeals to Walter White about crime is that it provides an escape from the drudgery of a 9 to 5 job and reality. The great irony of Walter working in the underground superlab of Gus Fring is that this merely replicates the drudgery of a 9 to 5 job.

(71) Walter White uses ricin to poison Lydia. This is

obviously a real poison. It was sometimes used by the KGB to kill people. What makes ricin a good method for a poisoner is that there are no immediate symptoms and it takes time to have effect. This gives the poisoner plenty of time to get away. Walter poisons Lydia by switching the Stevia she puts in her chamomile tea with ricin. The poison is less effective in a large amount of liquid and in reality it would have taken more ricin than Walter uses to actually kill Lydia.

(72) The lowest rated episode of Breaking Bad on IMDB is Fly with a score 7.9. By the standards of most other television shows though 7.9 is a pretty good score.

(73) The original concept for Better Call Saul is that it was going to be a half-hour show with a comedic slant that revolved around all the crazy characters who come into Saul's office each week seeking legal help. In the end it obviously morphed into something very different.

(74) Colin Hanks, an actor who happens to be the son of Tom Hanks, auditioned to play Jesse Pinkman. Colin Hanks has appeared in shows like Dexter.

(75) Walter is offered a way out of crime and his financial woes fairly early in the show when Gretchen and Elliott offer him a job with the company he helped form (but left after selling his shares). Walter's pride prevents him from taking the job. He doesn't want to be a charity case. There is a deeper factor too though in why Walter doesn't take this job. He is attracted to the world of crime because it offers him an excitement and sense of being alive that he has never experienced before.

(76) The mangled pink teddy bear with the missing eye rather foreshadows the fate of Gus Fring.

(77) Vince Galligan said that when they wrote the finale for season four they still didn't know at the time if they would be allowed to do a season five. The future of the show was by no means certain.

(78) El Camino: A Breaking Bad Movie was originally going to end with Jesse being arrested on the Canadian border but Vince Gilligan decided it would be too much of a downer if Jesse didn't get away and have the chance of a new life.

(79) Breaking Bad plainly takes some influence from Reservoir Dogs when it comes to character names. Reservoir Dogs has characters called Mr White and Mr Pink.

(80) Walter White was a chemistry teacher at J. P. Wynne High School. Vince Gillgan got his name from his elementary school - which was named J.P. Wynne Campus School.

(81) There are an estimated 270 deaths through the course of Breaking Bad.

(82) Todd Alquist is one of the most disturbing characters in Breaking Bad in that he is decent and ordinary on the surface, even coming across as gentle and polite, and yet in reality is a cold-blooded killer who will even murder a child without a moment of hesitation and then show no remorse whatsoever. This is what separates Jesse from Todd. Jesse has done terrible things but they haunt him because he has human emotions like guilt, regret, empathy, and compassion. Todd has none of these human emotions. He's basically a tabula rasa who will do anything that his uncle tells him to.

(83) Lydia Rodarte-Quayle is a business executive and the head of Logistics at Madrigal Electromotive GmbH. She is based in Houston and secretly in cahoots with Gus Fring. Lydia later works with Walter White and even Jack's gang of neo-Nazis.

(84) Giancarlo Esposito went to military school. He said that experience helped him to play Gus because in military school you have to take care of your clothes and be impeccably turned out. Gus is someone who takes pride in being smartly dressed and well presented.

(85) The background of Saul Goodman is that he was a scam artist named Jimmy McGill always getting into trouble. He then got a job in the mail room for his brother Chuck's law firm. Jimmy decided to train to be a lawyer like his brother and passed a correspondence course. Chuck, who knows Jimmy better than anyone, is plainly not thrilled about his brother becoming a lawyer. Chuck can see this is a potential recipe for disaster.

(86) Walter White is a very clever man but he makes some bad decisions as Heisenberg which lead to much chaos, death, the disintegration of his family, and eventually his own downfall. This was obviously a key component of the story because what would a high school chemistry teacher really know about crime, drug cartels, and gangs? Walter is often in over his head trying to get a foothold in the meth business.

(87) Walt makes thermite in Breaking Bad by taking the aluminum powder from an Etch A Sketch. Etch A Sketch is a mechanical drawing toy that was invented in the 1950s. It consists of a flat gray screen in a red plastic frame, with two knobs that control a stylus that moves horizontally or vertically and etches lines on the screen.

(88) The GPS co-ordinates in the show for where Walter's money is stashed were actually the co-ordinates for the studio where the production of Breaking Bad was based.

(89) Jesse's alias as a meth producer is Cap'n Cook.

(90) Better Call Saul seems to confirm that Gus Fring was gay - something which the producers confirmed too in the press. It seems likely that Max, the business partner of Gus who Hector Salamanca murdered, was more than just a business partner to Gus. A dominating motivation for Gus in his calculating war on the cartel and desire to punish Hector is revenge and justice for Max.

(91) In 2023, a poll by leading critics (from IndieWire, Variety, The Hollywood Reporter, USA Today, The A.V. Club, Forbes, The New York Times and Rolling Stone) ranked Breaking Bad as the best television show of the 2010s. Its closest competitors were Mad Men, The Leftovers, Fleabag, Twin Peaks: The Return, and Game of Thrones.

(92) The watch that Jesse gives Walter as a gift is a Monaco model TAG Heuer. TAG Heuer is a Swiss luxury watchmaker known for its high-quality and innovative timepieces. The brand was founded in 1860 and has since become a prestigious name in the world of luxury watches.

(93) Long-term methamphetamine use can lead to a range of physical and psychological health problems, including severe dental issues (often referred to as "meth mouth"), skin sores, weight loss, and insomnia.

(94) Anna Gunn played Walter White's long-suffering wife Skyler White in Breaking Bad. A section of viewers,

for whatever reason (she nagged Walter, ordered Walt Jr's new car to be returned etc), did not like Skyler - which even led to online sites devoted to hatred of the character. In response to this, Anna Gunn wrote a New York Times op-ed in which she said she was saddened that a strong female character was so despised. Anna also said in interviews that she felt as if people didn't like her personally because of Breaking Bad - despite the fact she was merely an actor playing a character someone else had written.

(95) Stacey Ehrmantraut is the widow of Mike's late son. Stacey was not a character in Breaking Bad and was played by an uncredited extra in a brief appearance. Stacey Ehrmantraut is though a regular character in Better Call Saul and played by Kerry Condon.

(96) The translation of Los Pollos Hermanos is The Chicken Brothers. The fast food chain was created by Gus Fring and Max Arciniega.

(97) Hank makes his own home brewed beer at home in Breaking Bad - Schraderbräu. The actor Dean Norris teamed up with the Figueroa Mountain Brewing Co to produce this beer for real.

(98) Vince Gilligan said that it was very deliberate not to go beyond five seasons on Breaking Bad. They wanted to leave people wanting more and get out before anyone started complaining about the series 'jumping the shark' or outstaying its welcome.

(99) Jesse's friend Badger is a big fan of Babylon 5. Babylon 5 is a science fiction television series created by J. Michael Straczynski. It originally aired from 1994 to 1998 and is set on a space station located in neutral

territory in the distant future. The show follows the diverse group of characters who live and work on the station as they navigate political intrigue, interstellar conflicts, and encounters with alien species. Bryan Cranston appeared in Babylon 5.

(100) Giancarlo Esposito had never actually watched Breaking Bad when he was offered the part of Gus. They sent him DVDs so he could check the show out.

(101) Jesse is a fan of Ice Road Truckers. Ice Road Truckers is a reality television series that follows truck drivers as they navigate treacherous ice-covered roads in northern Canada and Alaska.

(102) Bob Odenkirk played the young con artist version of Jimmy in the Better Call Saul flashbacks. Odenkirk is clearly too old for these flashback scenes but it probably would have been too jarring to have another actor playing the younger Jimmy.

(103) We see Jesse playing the video game RAGE in a couple of Breaking Bad episodes. RAGE is a first-person shooter video game developed by id Software and published by Bethesda Softworks. It was released in 2011 for Microsoft Windows, PlayStation 3, and Xbox 360.

(104) It was Bob Odenkirk's idea for Saul Goodman to have a combover hairstyle.

(105) Aaron Paul said in 2023 that he and the cast of Breaking Bad don't get any payments from the show streaming on Netflix - which he described as 'insane'. He was on the SAG-AFTRA picket line with Bryan Cranston when he made the comments.

(106) Saul suggests to Walter White that he launder his money in a Laser Tag business. Walter is not too keen on this. Laser tag is a game where players use infrared lasers to tag opponents in a specially designed arena or playing field. Players wear vests or other equipment with sensors that register hits from the lasers. The goal of the game is to tag as many opponents as possible while avoiding being tagged yourself.

(107) Breaking Bad: Criminal Elements is a 2020 mobile game based on the hit television series Breaking Bad. In the game, players take on the role of a new recruit in Walter White's drug empire and must build their own criminal organization by recruiting and managing their own crew, manufacturing and selling drugs, and expanding their territory. This game got fairly mediocre reviews when it came out.

(108) Mark Margolis, who played Hector Salamanca in Breaking Bad and Better Call Saul, had a long and memorable career with many film and television credits. He was even in the cult horror film Christmas Evil. Christmas Evil (aka You Better Watch Out) was written and directed by Lewis Jackson. Four years after this film came out a movie called Silent Night, Deadly Night created a rumpus by depicting a murderous killer dressed as Santa Claus. The thing is though that Christmas Evil had already done this but elicited no such controversy - presumably because so few people saw the film! Christmas Evil is a vastly superior film to Silent Night, Deadly Night too. Christmas Evil is more of a psychological drama than a horror film - though it does have some slasher elements in the second half. This is a morbidly compelling film which will linger in the memory long after you've seen it.

(109) Todd is clearly smitten with Lydia Rodarte-Quayle in Breaking Bad. It's safe to say that Lydia has no feelings at all for Todd though.

(110) Badger's real name is Brandon Mayhew.

(111) Laura Fraser, who played Lydia Rodarte-Quayle in Breaking Bad and Better Call Saul, is from Scotland in real life. Fraser has appeared in many films and television shows including Doctor Who and A Knight's Tale. She was also in the enjoyable Patrick Stewart version of A Christmas Carol.

(112) Larry Hankin played Old Joe, the salvage yard owner, in Breaking Bad. Hankin was considered for the part of Kramer in Seinfeld. He obviously didn't get that role but he did appear in Seinfeld as another character (who was auditioning to play Kramer in the episode).

(113) Several other cast members from Breaking Bad appeared in Seinfeld. They include Bryan Cranston, Anna Gunn, and Bob Odenkirk.

(114) Bob Odenkirk said that Saul Goodman was partly based on his first agent Ari Emanuel. Bob said that Hollywood agents tend to talk really fast and are very persuasive - which are two qualities that a lawyer like Saul would need to have.

(115) In season five of Breaking Bad, Walt wants Jack to kill the witnesses the DEA is trying to question. Jack comments that 'whacking' Osama bin Laden wasn't this complicated. This is a slight goof because season five takes place in 2010 and Osama bin Laden wasn't killed until 2011.

(116) Walter's habit of cutting crusts off his sandwiches was a consequence of Krazy-8, the first person Walt killed, doing this.

(117) Bob Odenkirk's background was in comedy. He was a writer on Saturday Night Live and the Late Night With Conan O'Brien. He then appeared in the 90s sketch series Mr Show. Bob Odenkirk went on to show that he was much more than a comedian or comic actor.

(118) Walter White and his wife end up buying the car wash business where Walter once worked in order to launder the money he has earned from producing meth. Money laundering is the process of disguising the origins of illegally obtained money, typically by transferring it through a complex web of transactions or investments. This is done in order to make the money appear to have been earned through legitimate means and to avoid detection or suspicion by law enforcement agencies

(119) Jonathan Banks said that one thing he would have liked to have seen (but didn't) in Breaking Bad or Better Call Saul was an appearance by the mother of Mike's late son Matt.

(120) Rian Johnson directed three episodes of Breaking Bad, including Ozymandias. Johnson would later direct, among other things, the Star Wars film The Last Jedi.

(121) RJ Mitte had to learn how to walk with crutches to play Walt Jr because he didn't use them in real life.

(122) Betsy Brandt, who played Marie, was pregnant when production of season two of Breaking Bad began. They had to hide this in the show obviously.

(123) In the episode Problem Dog the young man named Ben at Jesse's addiction group is a character we saw as one of Walter's school students in season one.

(124) The meth Jesse makes at the cartel superlab is 96.2% pure. This is impressive but not quite as pure as Walter White's meth.

(125) Dean Norris has joked about being typecast as law enforcement officers. He has played a lot of them in his career.

(126) Todd Alquist is noticeably heavier in El Camino than the character was in Breaking Bad - despite the fact that Todd's scenes in both productions are part of the same timeline. The reason why Todd looks different in El Camino is that Jesse Plemons had put weight on for his role in the film Black Mass.

(127) In 2011, Breaking Bad was added to Netflix. This gave the show a huge boost because Netflix subscribers who had not previously watching Breaking Bad binged the show and talked about how great it was. It was a new discovery for them.

(128) The first acting credit of Jonathan Banks was a 1970 educational short called Linda's Film on Menstruation.

(129) Walter starts driving a Volvo after killing Gus and drinking ice with Scotch after killing Mike. As with cutting his crusts off sandwiches after killing Krazy 8, these are weird and interesting little quirks where Walter seems to be taking on a trait of a victim.

(130) Breaking Bad was shot at Albuquerque Studios, a movie studio located at 5650 University Boulevard SE in

Albuquerque, New Mexico. In 2018 this studio was purchased by Netflix and expanded. They used it for some of the production of Stranger Things 4. Better Call Saul and El Camino: A Breaking Bad Movie also made use of this studio.

(131) The shooting location for the snow frosted New Hampshire cabin where Walter is hiding near the end of Breaking Bad was the Sandia Mountains of New Mexico.

(132) Robin Lord Taylor auditioned for the part of Todd Alquist before Jesse Plemons was cast. Robin Lord Taylor would later become known for his role as Oswald Cobblepot in the Fox TV series Gotham.

(133) Marie references Lone Wolf McQuade during a conversation with Hank in season five. Lone Wolf McQuade is a 1983 action film starring Chuck Norris as the title character, a tough Texas Ranger who prefers to work alone. The film follows McQuade as he takes on a dangerous drug lord and his gang.

(134) Gus Fring may have been partly inspired by Salvatore Testa. Salvatore "Chicken Man" Testa was an Italian-American mobster who was associated with the Philadelphia crime family. He earned the nickname "Chicken Man" due to his involvement in a lucrative poultry business that served as a front for illegal activities. Salvatore Testa was killed in 1984 while awaiting trial, in what was believed to be a hit in order to prevent him testifying in the court case.

(135) In Spanish, "felina" means feline or cat-like.

(136) The Jesse character was called Dupree in the original pilot script.

(137) Mark Margolis said he enjoyed playing Hector Salamanca because he didn't have many lines to learn!

(138) RJ Mitte had to do five auditions to get the part of Walt Jr.

(139) Todd's later ringtone in Breaking Bad is Lydia the Tattooed Lady. Lydia the Tattooed Lady (by Harold Arlen and E.Y. Harburg) is a comic song that Groucho Marx (as J. Cheever Loophole) sings in the 1939 Marx Brothers film At the Circus. Todd's ringtone is obviously in tribute to Lydia Rodarte-Quayle.

(140) Hank Schrader comes across as a super confident and extrovert man at the start of Breaking Bad but this is something of a front. We see in Breaking Bad that he suffers from anxiety and secretly has doubts about his own abilities. Hank is promoted and transferred to the El Paso, Texas DEA office but his harrowing experiences there cause him to suffer from PTSD. Despite his problems though (not least of which is being shot and having to learn to walk again) we see that Hank is an excellent detective and very shrewd. He is also unfailingly brave - especially in the dignified and defiant way that he faces death.

(141) Vince Gilligan said he loves the fan theory that Breaking Bad and The Walking Dead take place in the same universe and it was actually Walter's blue meth which caused the zombie epidemic!

(142) A couple of replicas of the RV used by Jesse and Walter in the show were preserved. Typically on a production you will have back-up vehicles in case one is damaged or breaks down.

(143) Mike Ehrmantraut is hired by Daniel Wormald ("Pryce") to protect him during a drug deal with Nacho Varga early in Better Call Saul. Mike impresses in the audition - despite the fact that he is the only person who hasn't brought a gun or weapon. The only thing Mike has packed is a pimento cheese sandwich (which we know from Breaking Bad is a favorite sandwich of Mike). Pimento cheese is a type of spread or dip made from cheddar cheese, mayonnaise, pimentos, and various seasonings. It is popular in the Southern United States and is often served as a sandwich filling, cracker topping, or vegetable dip.

(144) Vince Gilligan said that he put something of his own personality into Walt. Not the meth producing/criminal stuff obviously (!) but more Walt before he became Heisenberg.

(145) In the finale Felina, Walter White listens to the song El Paso by Marty Robbins. The song is from the perspective of a cowboy smitten with a young Mexican dancer named Feleena.

(146) Vince Gillgan said that he considered having Skyler commit suicide in the show but the other writers didn't think this was a good idea.

(147) It is probably fair to say that the character of Saul Goodman - while still no boy scout - is made more sympathetic and likeable in Better Call Saul compared to Breaking Bad. Saul is a sleaze with no morals in Breaking Bad and although he does plenty of bad things in Better Call Saul the character is more nuanced and seems to have more of a conscience. Of course, in Better Call Saul he spends most of the series as Jimmy. He only becomes Saul Goodman very late in the show.

(149) Penn Badgley was strongly considered for the part of Jesse Pinkman. In the end it was between Badgley and Aaron Paul and they obviously went with the latter. Penn Badgley said he was sad not to get the part because the Breaking Bad pilot was the best script he had ever read.

(150) Robert Forster, who played Ed Galbraith, sadly died on the day that El Camino: A Breaking Bad Movie was released. It was one of the very last things that he did.

(151) Walter White attended the California Institute of Technology. The California Institute of Technology, commonly known as Caltech, is a private research university located in Pasadena, California. It is known for its strengths in science and engineering, particularly in the fields of physics, chemistry, biology, and computer science. Caltech was founded in 1891 and has a strong emphasis on research and innovation.

(152) In the last ever Breaking Bad scene, the blood smudge on the chemical tank left by Walter White is in the shape of a W.

(153) Breaking Bad is a Southern slang term meaning to turn to a life of crime or deviancy.

(154) Chuck McGill in Better Call Saul suffers from Electromagnetic hypersensitivity. Electromagnetic hypersensitivity, also known as electromagnetic sensitivity or electrohypersensitivity, is a condition in which individuals experience physical symptoms when they are exposed to electromagnetic fields (EMFs) generated by electronic devices such as cell phones, Wi-Fi routers, and power lines. Symptoms can include headaches, fatigue, dizziness, skin irritation, and difficulty concentrating. There is ongoing debate within

the scientific community about whether electromagnetic hypersensitivity is a real condition or if it is a psychological phenomenon and all in the mind.

(155) Hank takes to collecting minerals when he is recovering at home after being shot in Breaking Bad. Mineral collecting is actually quite a popular hobby. A collection of solid minerals is known as a rock. There are three main types of rock - sedimentary, igneous, metamorphic.

(156) Leonel and Marco Salamanca, the Terminator like cartel enforcers, are played by Daniel and Luis Moncada. Daniel and Luis are brothers in real life.

(157) Bill Burr got his part as Patrick Kuby in Breaking Bad because he was a big fan of the show and reached out for a part.

(158) Gus Fring will rarely have an associate come to his house as a guest but when he does he will cook them Paila marina. Paila marina is a traditional Chilean seafood soup or light stew usually served in a paila. It usually contains a shellfish stock base cooked with different kinds of shellfish and fish.

(159) We see in an episode of Breaking Bad that Walter White and his son are fans of the grilled cheese sandwich. Walt serves the grilled cheese with potato chips.

(160) When the show was still in production, Vince Gilligan said he avoiding reading anything Breaking Bad related online because he wanted tunnel vision until the show finished.

(161) Anna Gunn said and she and Betsy Brandt had a

backstory that Skylar and Marie had a difficult childhood. This explained their close but slightly dysfunctional bond as adults.

(162) Michael Slovis was the director of photography on Breaking Bad from season two. Slovis said that Vince Gilligan mentioned two films in relation to how he wanted the show to look - The Good, The Bad, and the Ugly and The French Connection. The former is a classic and epic spaghetti Western by Sergio Leone and the latter is a 1970s crime thriller directed by William Friedkin.

(163) Bryan Cranston wore a bald cap for his scene in El Camino: A Breaking Bad Movie. He couldn't shave his head because he was appearing in a play on Broadway.

(164) The German company Madrigal Electromotive GmbH is obviously fictional. GmbH is an abbreviation for "Gesellschaft mit beschränkter Haftung," which is a type of legal entity commonly used in Germany and other German-speaking countries. It is similar to a limited liability company (LLC) in other countries and provides limited liability to its owners, known as shareholders. GmbHs are often used for small to medium-sized businesses and can be formed with just one shareholder and a minimum share capital. Madrigal executives are partners with Gus Fring and help him with equipment he might need.

(165) Raymond Cruz said he found it hard work playing the volatile and crazy Tuco Salamanca in Breaking Bad. Cruz was apparently more than happy for Tuco to be killed off. He did reprise the role though for two episodes of Better Call Saul and for a 2023 Superbowl commercial for PopCorners - which also featured Bryan Cranston and Aaron Paul as Walter and Jesse. Tuco was supposed to be

an antagonist for Walter and Jesse for longer in Breaking Bad but these plans were abandoned due to Cruz being cast in The Closer.

(166) Charlie Collier, who was a bigwig at AMC at the time, was the person who saw potential in Breaking Bad and called Vince Gilligan in for a meeting. Rob Sorcher, who ran the AMC channel, had suggested Collier read the pilot script for Breaking Bad because he loved it.

(167) Aaron Paul said he had run out of money when he got the part of Jesse Pinkman. The role arrived just in the nick of time.

(168) Bryan Cranston said it was his idea that early on Walter's clothes would sort of blend into the White family wallpaper - as if he was invisible. Walter White is milquetoast central when we first meet him.

(169) Vince Gilligan described Walter White as having the worst mid-life crisis in history!

(170) Bryan Cranston said he found shooting the scene where Walter watches Jane die quite distressing and difficult because he had a teenage daughter in real life.

(171) The only characters to have all appeared in Breaking Bad, Better Call Saul, and El Camino: A Breaking Bad Movie are Ed Galbraith, Austin Ramey, Walter White, Mike Ehrmantraut, and Jesse Pinkman.

(172) Walter and Jesse initially use pseudoephedrine as a precursor chemical to cook methamphetamine. Pseudoephedrine is a decongestant medication commonly used to relieve nasal congestion caused by allergies, colds, or hay fever. When they run out of this

chemical, Walter and Jesse steal methylamine from a factory to use as part of a process to synthesize methamphetamine. Methylamine is a naturally occurring compound that is found in small amounts in certain foods and in the environment. It is also a chemical that is used in various industrial processes, such as in the production of pharmaceuticals, pesticides, and plastics.

(173) Although he isn't making that much money as a high school chemistry teacher and his chemo/treatment bills are going to be expensive, we see that Walter does still have a choice not to go into crime - despite the fact he acts as if he doesn't. He could have taken the job from Elliott and Gretchen and let them pay for his treatment. He could have found some other way - as financially difficult as it might have been. Walter is plainly drawn to crime and his new secret life. It almost becomes like a weird form of role play for Walt that allows him to escape from reality and his mundane life.

(174) One of Giancarlo Esposito's early roles was as Mickey in seven episodes of Sesame Street!

(175) The alias Heisenberg obviously refers to Werner Heisenberg. Werner Heisenberg was a German physicist who is best known for his contributions to the development of quantum mechanics. He is perhaps most famous for his uncertainty principle, which states that the more precisely the position of a particle is known, the less precisely its momentum can be known, and vice versa. He was awarded the Nobel Prize in Physics in 1932 for his work in this field. Heisenberg also played a key role in the development of nuclear physics and was involved in the German nuclear weapons program during World War II. After the war, he worked to promote peaceful uses of nuclear energy and advocated for international

cooperation in scientific research.

(176) Todd tries to learn how to cook pure Walter White style meth in Breaking Bad but he never quite manages to get there. According to Lydia, the best batch made by Todd was only 76% pure.

(177) The main reason why Bryan Cranston wanted Heisenberg to wear a hat was that he was worried about his shaved head burning in the New Mexico sunshine and getting cold during night/winter shoots.

(178) Jesse Pinkman and Walt Jr never actually meet each other in Breaking Bad.

(179) There were vague plans at one point for Saul Goodman to die at the end of Breaking Bad. In the end they obviously decided not to do this.

(180) There is a lot of Breaking Bad 'merch' online. You can even buy a Mike Ehrmantraut toy figure.

(181) The episode Face Off - which is perfect with its double meaning - probably had its title inspired by the John Woo film Face/Off. Face/Off is a 1997 action thriller film starring John Travolta and Nicolas Cage. The plot revolves around an FBI agent and a terrorist who undergo a face transplant surgery to assume each other's identity in order to stop a terrorist plot.

(182) In the opening episode of season five (Live Free or Die), a flashfoward features Walter White in a diner. When he goes out to his car we see that he has a M60 machine gun in the trunk. At the time, Vince Galligan actually had no idea why Walter needed a machine gun or what he planned to use it for. It was something Vince had

to figure out later.

(183) Steven Gomez, Hank's Drug Enforcement Administration partner and friend, was another character who was originally supposed to die in the first season. A writer's strike is credited with saving Gomez and Jesse Pinkman from an early bath in the show. The original plans for season one were reworked somewhat - with the planned early deaths removed from the story.

(184) Vince Gilligan said the writer's strike was a blessing in disguise because he was 'burning' through the story on Breaking Bad too quickly. The pause allowed him to take stock and adjust the pacing of the show's story arcs. Plus of course it saved numerous characters from being bumped off!

(185) Saul Goodman's real name is James Morgan McGill. He liked people to call him Jimmy rather than James.

(186) The RV used in the show was purchased from a husband and wife who had driven it all over America.

(187) Krysten Ritter had a fake plastic chest prosthetic for Jane's death scene. This was necessary because she could not be seen to be breathing and Jesse also had to pound on her chest.

(188) There were incidents of real life meth dealers adding blue dye to the drug when Breaking Bad became a hit in order to make their product seem more high grade.

(189) Gus Fring drives a humble Volvo station wagon. This is obviously a very deliberate choice of vehicle. Gus doesn't want to attract any attention.

(190) You see a few times in the show that Gale Boetticher has some Ron Paul stickers. Ron Paul is a former politician who takes a libertarian view on economic, social, and geopolitical matters.

(191) Vince Gilligan said the idea behind the show was to watch a man (Walter White) turn from 'Mr Chips to Scarface'. Goodbye, Mr. Chips is a novella by James Hilton, first published in 1934. It tells the story of Mr. Chipping, a beloved and long-serving teacher.

(192) Gus Fring mentions in Breaking Bad that his children are fussy eaters and so he rarely gets a chance to cook traditional Chilean dishes at home. We also see toys at his house. However, we never see his kids or a wife. It is left ambiguous as to whether Gus really does have a wife or children. It seems plausible that Gus, even if he was gay (which the producers later confirmed), would marry so as to pose as a family man and 'fit in' more. It appears more likely though that Gus wasn't actually married. A third possibility is that he got divorced.

(193) Vince Gilligan said a surprising influence on Breaking Bad was Frosty the Snowman. Both Frosty and Walter White only seem to take on their true persona when they wear a hat. Frosty the Snowman is a television cartoon by Rankin/Bass which runs to about 25 minutes. It's quite a simple cartoon in terms of animation but has plenty of charm and has become a Christmas favorite. Most people remember this cartoon because of the unmistakable voice of Jimmy Durante as the narrator.

(194) Vince Gilligan admitted that Aaron Paul's Hollywood teeth as Jesse strain credibility somewhat in Breaking Bad. Jesse has taken a lot of meth (and other drugs), lived rough at times, and also taken his share of

beatings so in reality his teeth would probably be in terrible shape.

(195) The meth used in the show was actually made out of rock candy.

(196) Saul Goodman/Jimmy got his law degree through a correspondence course with the University of American Samoa. This university is fictional and doesn't actually exist.

(197) Jesse uses the words 'Yo!' and 'Bitch' a lot. Aaron Paul said 95% of these were in the script and he only improvised a few extra ones.

(198) The scenes which are set in Germany in Breaking Bad were actually shot in New Mexico.

(199) Giancarlo Esposito came up with the idea that Gus Fring would straighten his tie just before he dropped dead.

(200) Albuquerque is the largest city in the state of New Mexico. It is known for its rich cultural heritage, diverse population, and stunning desert landscape.

(201) Vince Gilligan said that Sony Pictures thought that Breaking Bad was not a great title for the show and wanted it changed. He stuck to his guns though and kept the title.

(202) Laura Fraser said that playing Lydia Rodarte-Quayle in Breaking Bad was a huge boost for her career because she used to have do endless auditions but after Breaking Bad she was suddenly being offered parts without having to audition.

(203) Bob Odenkirk played an agent on The Larry Sanders Show - which was a brilliant 1990s comedy about a chat show host (memorably played by the late Garry Shandling). It was apparently The Larry Sanders Show which gave Vince Gilligan the idea of casting Bob Odenkirk as Saul Goodman.

(204) David Costabile, who played Gale Boetticher, was already a fan of Breaking Bad and desperate to be in the show.

(205) Victor Bravenec, the senior chemist of DEA's South Central Laboratory, in Dallas, was an advisor on Breaking Bad and helped them get the RV meth lab accurate. Bravenec had to come up with something that a scientist like Walt would create - as opposed to your average meth producer on the street.

(206) Jesse Pinkman was created by Vince Gilligan as a 'plot mechanism' to introduce Walter to the world of crime and meth. The character would though become much more important to the show than originally anticipated.

(207) In the scene where Walter and Jesse are trapped in the RV and Hank is trying to get in, Hank runs a tire iron along the side to intimidate the occupants. It was actually Bryan Cranston who came up with this suggestion.

(208) Don Juan Bolsa (played by Javier Grajeda) is the co-founder of the cartel in Breaking Bad. Bolsa often finds himself acting as the bridge between the Salamancas and Gus Fring. He has to play diplomat to keep the peace.

(209) The 'hazard pay' for the employees of Gus Fring is in the Craddock Marine Bank. This is an X-Files joke as

the Craddock Marine Bank was used by Fox Mulder.

(210) Vince Gilligan said Fly was one of his favorite episodes. He described Fly as a bit like Breaking Bad meets Waiting for Godot.

(211) Gus Fring became the primary villain of Breaking Bad because the writers were so impressed with Giancarlo Esposito. It was such a great performance that it seemed stupid not to expand his part.

(212) Saul Goodman has gaudy fake plastic Ionian columns in his office. Ionian columns are a type of ancient Greek architectural column characterized by fluted shafts, a base, and a capital with volutes or scrolls.

(213) Bryan Cranston is apparently a big fan of Breaking Bad fan art.

(214) Howard Hamlin (played by Patrick Fabian) is the boss of law firm Hamlin, Hamlin & McGill (HHM) in Better Call Saul. The firm was established by Jimmy/Saul's brother Chuck and Howard's father. Howard becomes something of an arch nemesis for Jimmy in Better Call Saul although whether Howard quite deserves all of this hate is certainly open to question.

(215) Vince Gilligan said the key to ending a show is making sure you don't leave any 'loose ends' which might make the final resolution unsatisfying.

(216) Aaron Paul and Giancarlo Esposito both later appeared in the HBO show Westworld.

(217) Walter White was apparently a hotshot in

crystallography as a young man. Crystallography is the scientific study of the arrangement of atoms within crystalline solids. It involves the use of X-ray diffraction, electron diffraction, and other techniques to determine the geometric structure of crystals.

(218) Jesse Pinkman's signature is to add chili powder to his methamphetamine. Walter White and Tuco Salamanca are not very impressed by this.

(219) The plane crash in Breaking Bad may have taken some inspiration from Aeroméxico Flight 498. Aeroméxico Flight 498 was a flight from Mexico City to Los Angeles that crashed on August 31, 1986, in Cerritos, California. The crash was caused by a mid-air collision with a small private aircraft, killing all 64 people on board the Aeroméxico flight as well as 3 people on the private plane and 15 people on the ground. The name of the air-traffic controller in this real life incident just happened to be Walter White.

(220) In the Better Call Saul episode titled Magic Man, we see Jimmy (as Gene) ask Ed Galbraith for an adaptor rather than a dust filter for his vacuum. This is code for Jimmy needing to be relocated again - a service which Ed tells him will cost double the usual fee.

(221) The Terminator like cartel cousins wear skull tipped boots in Breaking Bad. These boots identify them as cartel members but might also reference Santa Muerte. Santa Muerte or "Holy Death," is a popular folk saint in Mexican and Latino-American cultures. She is often depicted as a skeletal figure, similar to the Grim Reaper.

(222) The VisitAlbuquerque.org website has an entire page dedicated to Breaking Bad and what the show meant

to the city (and indeed what the city meant to the cast and crew).

(223) In the Better Call Saul scene which features Saul and Walter in Ed Galbraith's basement we learn that Walter White thinks time travel is impossible.

(224) You see some characters in Breaking Bad, including Saul and Gus, wear blue ribbons in the show. These ribbons are in memory of those who died in the plane crash.

(225) There are a few scenes in season one where Bryan Cranston wore a wig because he had already shaved his head but they needed a pre-shaved head Walter scene.

(226) A number of different real locations were used to depict the exterior of the school Walter White teaches at. They included Rio Rancho High School and Eldorado High School.

(227) According to U.S Customs data, methamphetamine is their second most seized drug in terms of volume.

(228) There was a DVD box-set called the Breaking Bad: The Complete Series Barrel - which came with a Los Pollos Hermanos apron and a commemorative challenge coin designed by Vince Gilligan. You can find this on Amazon - though it probably won't be cheap.

(229) After the last episode of Breaking Bad, there was a lot of debate over whether Walter White actually survived or not. El Camino rather put this debate to rest.

(230) The famous film director Guillermo del Toro said he desperately wanted to direct the Breaking Bad episode

Ozymandias. He obviously lost out to Rian Johnson.

(231) Bob Odenkirk said he is obviously nothing like Jimmy/Saul in real life. Bob describes himself as thoughtful and cautious whereas Jimmy/Saul is impetuous and often allows his darker instincts to drive him.

(232) Dean Norris said he enjoyed his cameo in Better Call Saul because he was playing Hank in his 'prime before the PTSD'.

(233) Giancarlo Esposito said that his own unofficial backstory for Gus Fring is that Gus was a military officer in Chile and became quite powerful.

(234) For those familiar with Game of Thrones, Todd's control of Jesse in El Camino, how he has him so broken that he persuades Jesse to put down a gun, rather evoked the Ramsey Bolton/Theon relationship.

(235) Bryan Cranston said he doesn't think or worry about the fact that Breaking Bad is an impossible act to follow and he'll probably never be in anything that good again.

(236) If you look on Rotten Tomatoes you can find some of the original 2008 reviews of Breaking Bad when it first started (though if you try to go to the publications through the links nearly all of them have failed to archive their review or removed it). While the early reviews are generally pretty good you'll see that The Boston Globe, New Yorker, Chicago Tribune, Seattle Post-Intelligencer, Pittsburgh Post-Gazette, and Boston Herald all gave Breaking Bad a negative review and expressed doubts it would last very long. The Boston Herald even called the

show 'tedious' - which is pretty amazing when you consider Breaking Bad is one of the most binged shows in television history. Suffice to say, you shouldn't always listen to critics when a new show begins.

(237) Aaron Paul released an app in 2014 called Yo, Bitch.

(238) Vince Gilligan said that pitching Breaking Bad to HBO was the worst meeting of his life. Vince said their disinterest was palpable and it was basically a waste of his time.

(239) Kelley Dixon was the Emmy winning editor on Breaking Bad and did many of the famous 'meth montages' She also worked on Better Call Saul. Kelley also hosted a podcast for the two shows.

(240) Vince Gilligan named the tortoise/head scene in Negro Y Azul as one of his top five Breaking Bad highlights.

(241) Aaron Paul has said he didn't think his Breaking Bad audition was very good. It all turned out fine in the end as he got the part anyway.

(242) In the episode Gray Matter, Walter and Skylar go to a swanky birthday party For Elliott Schwartz. Walter tells some of his old colleagues that he went into education and they ask what college he is at. Needless to say this all humiliating for Walter. The question of how a brilliant scientist like Walter ended up teaching at a high school is left unanswered.

(243) The actress Ali MacGraw shot a cameo for Gray Matter but it was cut out of the episode. She played herself and was going to be a guest at Elliott's birthday

party.

(244) The gun that Jesse purchases in the episode Seven Thirty-Seven is a Ruger SP101 handgun.

(245) The name Los Pollos Hermanos seems likely inspired by El Pollo Loco. El Pollo Loco ("The Crazy Chicken") is an independent restaurant chain serving Mexican-style grilled chicken. Juan Francisco Ochoa established the first El Pollo Loco restaurant in Guasave, Sinaloa, Mexico in 1974.

(246) A flashback in Breaking Bad shows us a younger Walt and Skylar viewing the house that they later live in. Walt is not convinced that the house is big enough. This tells us two things about Walt. He expects to wealthy and he expects to have a big family.

(247) The scene in the Better Call Saul episode Saul Gone where Saul and Walter are in Ed Galbraith's bunker was actually intended for Breaking Bad but there was never enough time to film it.

(248) Bob Odenkirk said he tried to appear a bit out of breath in Breaking Bad during some scenes because Saul Goodman is not a man who takes care of himself very well. He drinks too much and eats a lot of takeaway food.

(249) Vince Gilligan said he didn't get a grasp on the character of Walter White until the episode Gray Matter. It was only when he came up with the idea that Elliott Schwartz would offer to solve all of Walt's problems at a stroke but Walt would refuse because of his pride and ego that he felt he finally understood Walter White.

(250) You see a pack of Morley cigarettes in the first ever

Breaking Bad episode. This is a fictional brand that was used in The X-Files (and other shows too).

(251) Walter White's underwear from the first episode sold for $9,900 at a 2013 auction.

(252) Gus Fring's secret superlab was capable of producing 300 pounds of meth a week. 300 pounds of meth would be worth about $4 million on the street.

(253) The longest episode of Breaking Bad is actually Pilot - which clocks in at 58 minutes.

(254) The longest episode of Better Call Saul is Saul Gone - which clocks in at 69 minutes.

(255) After the end of Breaking Bad, Bryan Cranston told his agent that he would not consider another television role for at least three years.

(256) Dean Norris said he went out with Aaron Paul in Albuquerque a lot shooting Breaking Bad but that Bryan Cranston didn't go out much and is more the type of person who prefers a quiet night indoors.

(257) El Camino in Spanish basically means 'the way' or the 'path'.

(258) The real location uased for Mike's house in Breaking Bad was 204 Edith Blvd, NE, Albuquerque.

(259) Breaking Bad is arguably the greatest example of 'sticking the landing' when it comes to famous television shows. The episodes which wrapped up the show are considered to be Breaking Bad firing on all cylinders. This has assuredly not been the case with other famous shows

though. The endings of both Lost and Game of Thrones were so mediocre that many fans of both of those shows are still annoyed about it to this day.

(260) The red in Bryan Cranston's hair was dyed a browner shade early in Breaking Bad because they didn't want Walter to be a man who stood out in any way.

(261) The richest cast member of Breaking Bad, as of 2024, is apparently Bryan Cranston with a net wealth of $40 million.

(262) In real life, Anna Gunn and Betsy Brandt (who play Skylar and Marie) are actually taller than Aaron Paul, Jonathan Banks, Dean Norris, Giancarlo Esposito, and Raymond Cruz.

(263) In his younger years, before he was famous, Aaron Paul did commercials for Juicy Fruit, Corn Pops, and Vanilla Coke.

(264) Badger's Star Trek synopsis in Breaking Bad was later turned into an animation. Vince Gilligan and Peter Gould said they are both closet Trekkies so it was easy for them to write dialogue where a drug addled Badger makes up his own Star Trek story.

(265) In an article on Indie Wire discussing the best and worst television prequels, nearly all of the contributors cited Better Call Saul as the best television prequel. Other prequels which drew praised were Hannibal and Bates Motel. As for the worst television prequels, barbs were directed at Star Trek: Enterprise, Fear the Walking Dead, and Gotham.

(266) Dean Norris said that Hank's death scene was done

in one take.

(267) The shooting location for Tuco's headquarters in Breaking Bad was above a coffee shop called Java Joe's.

(268) Bob Odenkirk said that on Breaking Bad he had no idea what Saul Goodman did when he wasn't in his office. He presumed that Saul probably played golf and went to strip clubs at the weekend. In the spin-off show Better Call Saul we see that Jimmy/Saul is a much more complex man than we suspected.

(269) Bryan Cranston said he only became aware Breaking Bad was a big deal when the production signs in Albuquerque directing cast and crew where to go started to be stolen as souvenirs.

(270) Dean Norris is another member of the Breaking Bad cast who was in The X-Files. Dean was in the episode titled F. Emasculata.

(271) Badger and Skinny Pete are fans of horror video games. They debate the zombie merits of Left 4 Dead, Call Of Duty Zombies and Resident Evil 4.

(272) Bryan Cranston is the godfather to Aaron Paul's son.

(273) Bob Odenkirk, who obviously has a background in comedy, said that doing drama is really hard work.

(274) Vince Gilligan directed the first episode of both Breaking Bad and Better Call Saul.

(275) Breaking Bad made use of some hand held camera work. When they made Better Call Saul they deliberately

eschewed this in order to give that show a different look.

(276) Bob Odenkirk was actually bankrupt at one point before he was cast in Breaking Bad.

(277) El Camino had its debut on Netflix and was then shown on AMC a few months later. This was an illustration of how much the television business had changed since Breaking Bad.

(278) Larry Hankin, who played old Joe in Breaking Bad, had retired from acting when El Camino was announced but he agreed to come out of retirement to shoot a scene.

(279) The original plan for El Camino was for it to be a short film. A sort of bonus mini-episode. It became much more than that in the end.

(280) Dan Wachsberger (played by Chris Freihofer) is the crooked lawyer that is in charge of the 'hazard pay' scheme Gus Fring left his men. Mike attempts to use Wachsberger to get money to his granddaughter. Wachsberger meets a grisly end when Walter employs Jack's gang to kill anyone connected to Fring.

(281) In the original concept for Breaking Bad, Hank was a trifle more abrasive and politically incorrect. This was toned down somewhat.

(282) Bryan Cranston received a star on the Hollywood Walk of Fame in 2013.

(283) You can, should you need one, now buy a Walter White fleece blanket.

(284) Dean Norris and Raymond Cruz both had small

roles in the 1990 film Gremlins 2: The New Batch.

(285) The kid (Drew) on the bike that Todd shoots in Dead Freight was played by Sam Webb. Sam Webb only has one IMDB credit since Breaking Bad so it seems he decided not to become an actor.

(286) We learn in Better Call Saul that the bodies of Lalo Salamanca and Howard Hamlin are buried in the Gus Fring superlab where Walter and Jesse work in Breaking Bad.

(287) Gus Fring's underground superlab cost him $8 million to construct. It turned out to be a good investment as he made considerably more than $8 million from the meth that Walter White and Jesse cooked up down there.

(288) The copy of Walt Whitman's Leaves Of Grass used in the show sold for $65,500 at a 2013 auction.

(289) According to the 2020 census, Albuquerque has 564,559 residents.

(290) Giancarlo Esposito said he found people were sometimes a bit wary of him in real life after he started playing Gus Fring!

(291) The Salamancas are basically the henchmen for the Juarez Cartel. This explains why they act as if they can do what they want.

(292) In the episode To'hajiilee there is a fictional car rental company called Lariat. This fictional car rental company was used in The X-Files.

(293) In his first scene in Breaking Bad, we learn that

Saul Goodman doesn't accept American Express. He prefers cash or a money order.

(294) Adam Godley, who played Elliott Schwartz, used to be in the show Suits. One of his co-stars in Suits was a certain Meghan Markle. David Costabile, who played Gale Boetticher, was also in Suits.

(295) According to Bryan Cranston, the original title for Breaking Bad was Hidden in Plain Sight.

(296) Breaking Bad was shot primarily on 35 mm film.

(297) Aaron Paul said that Raymond Cruz in real life is the 'kindest and sweetest' person you will ever meet. Thankfully then, he's nothing like Tuco!

(298) Bryan Cranston said in an interview that he hoped Breaking Bad would offer some 'illumination' to how poorly paid teachers are. He said Walter White working a second job at the car wash was based on real teachers having to get second jobs to pay the bills.

(299) When he was first offered the part of Saul Goodman, Bob Odenkirk suggested they should probably hire an actor who is Jewish in real life. They had to explain to Bob that Saul is really called Jimmy and he's of Irish descent. Saul Goodman is just a facade. Bob Odenkirk is of Irish descent himself.

(300) Laura Fraser was initially cast as Jessica Brody in the television show Homeland but then replaced by Morena Baccarin. Laura said she is happy this happened now because otherwise she wouldn't have been free to play Lydia in Breaking Bad.

(301) Jesse Pinkman seems to be fond of Nike sneakers.

(302) Bryan Cranston was 66 when he played Walter White in Better Call Saul.

(303) Robert Forster knew Bryan Cranston before Breaking Bad because they'd played some poker games together with other actors.

(304) Gus Fring is shown to be a very hands-on boss at Los Pollos Hermanos. We see him dealing with garbage and sweeping up. He even takes orders at the counter. Of course, this is all part of his deception. No one could ever suspect him of being a criminal if he's always seen working at Los Pollos Hermanos.

(305) The location for the Cinnabon in Omaha that Jimmy/Saul ends up working in as Gene is really Albuquerque's Cottonwood Mall.

(306) Lalo's real name is Eduardo Salamanca.

(307) Vince Gilligan and Peter Gould said they cast Robert Forster in Breaking Bad because they loved him so much in Jackie Brown.

(308) Bryan Cranston said he liked how Breaking Bad tested our loyalty to characters. For example, we find ourselves rooting for Mike and Jesse but also see them do bad things.

(309) Bryan Cranston shot his scene as Walter White in the Better Call Saul episode called Saul Gone many months in advance because they knew he would soon be unavailable due to other work.

(310) Peter Gould said he was slightly more sympathetic to Walter White than others because in real life he spent a number of years teaching and struggling to pay the bills. Peter of course did not though start cooking meth to make ends up and start killing people!

(311) RJ Mitte said that Walt Jr's personality was quite similar to what he was like in real life.

(312) There is a Breaking Bad Trivial Pursuit. The game has 600 questions.

(313) You can, should you desire one, now buy a Breaking Bad chopping board.

(314) When he recovers from his injuries, Hank drives a 2011 Dodge Durango.

(315) Vince Gilligan said he believes Walt Jr did indeed get the money from Elliott and Gretchen. He also believes that Walt Jr, despite his anger, missed his father after he was gone.

(316) Walt Jr's alias Flynn is inspired by Errol Flynn.

(317) The blurb that Los Pollos Hermanos use for their chicken is "slow-cooked to perfection... one taste, and you'll know."

(318) Vince Gilligan said it took him and the other writers about a year to decide how Breaking Bad should end.

(319) Badger and Skinny Pete do not appear in Better Call Saul.

(320) Vince Gilligan said Walter initially intending to kill

Jesse in the last season but changing his mind is based on The Searchers. The Searchers is a classic Western film released in 1956, directed by John Ford and starring John Wayne. The story follows Ethan Edwards, a Confederate veteran on a quest to find his niece, who has been kidnapped by Comanche Indians. Edwards plans to kill his niece but has second thoughts.

(321) When the last season of Breaking Bad began there was a fan theory that it would end with Skylar murdering Walter White.

(322) There are a smattering of Pulp Fiction references in Breaking Bad. This film was plainly an influence on the show.

(323) The only time the Breaking Bad theme is used within the show is the scene in the last episode where Walt watches Elliott and Gretchen on television and then the state troopers surround Walt's cabin.

(324) A rather downbeat fan theory is that the last episode was just a hallucination a dying Walt had in that New Hampshire cabin.

(325) Jimmy/Saul's favorite ice cream is mint choc chip.

(326) Hank's full name is Henry R. Schrader

(327) There is actually a Breaking Bad board game which is titled (as you might expect) Breaking Bad: The Board Game. The game has pretty good reviews online. The blurb goes like this - 'Based on the critically-acclaimed TV series, Breaking Bad: The Board Game propels you into the treacherous underbelly of Albuquerque, New Mexico. Will you play as a member of one of the criminal factions

(Heisenberg, Los Pollos Hermanos, or the Juarez Cartel), trying to amass a fortune by manufacturing the biggest stash of Blue Sky while eliminating your rivals? Or will you join the ranks of the Drug Enforcement Administration, ready to slap the cuffs on the lawbreakers who would dare peddle their poison in your city? In more detail, when playing a criminal faction, your goal is to produce Blue Sky, then sell the quantity needed to win before your opponents can. You can also win the game by taking out all of your opponents by using cards to bomb, shoot, or otherwise eliminate them. As the DEA agent, your goal is to seize the criminal factions' labs (by playing DEA Raid cards). You can also win the game by taking out all of your opponents, either by killing them or putting them in jail. In game terms, on their turn, a player takes two of the following actions: Draw a card. Play a card from their hand. Produce Blue Sky (dealer only). Sell 1 Blue Sky on their faction board (dealer only). Be the one who knocks.'

(328) Saul references Hogan's Heroes in season five. Hogan's Heroes is a television sitcom that originally aired on CBS from 1965 to 1971. The show was set in a German prisoner of war camp during World War II and followed the adventures of a group of Allied prisoners who used their wits and cunning to outsmart their German captors.

(329) Robert Forster described his character Ed Galbraith as a 'straight shooter'. Ed will tell it like it is.

(330) Giancarlo Esposito was in another popular show after Breaking Bad because he played Stan Edgar in The Boys.

(331) Saul Goodman/Jimmy McGill's last arc in the Breaking Bad universe feels vaguely inspired by Crime

and Punishment by Dostoevsky. Crime and Punishment is about a former student named Rodion Raskolnikov who is suffering from severe financial problems and ends up murdering a pawnbroker to rectify his money worries. Raskolnikov had rationalised the murder by telling himself that the pawnbroker was a bad person anyway and that with money he could now live a much better life and do some good with his new found wealth. He could, for example, help his family and save his sister from an unhappy marriage. However, Raskolnikov learns that murder and taking a life is not quite this simple. After the act is done and Raskolnikov has killed, he is wracked with guilt and disgust for his actions. His life and mental state soon begins to frazzle and descend into paranoia and confusion. Because of his extreme guilt, he finds that he can't enjoy the money he has stolen because it was not acquired through honest means. Although the world is apparently no poorer for lacking a heartless pawnbroker, Raskolnikov discovers that a criminal act as serious as murder preys on the mind and makes it impossible for him to move on with his life. He soon begins to have an urge to confess - the only way to clear his soul.

(332) You could argue there's a slight medical goof in Breaking Bad because when Walter is having chemotherapy he shouldn't be able to grow facial hair.

(333) Breaking Bad, along with The Sopranos, has been credited with popularizing the anti-hero genre in television.

(334) Hank seems to reference Shania Twain more than once in Breaking Bad. Shania Twain is a Canadian singer and songwriter who is known for her country and pop music.

(335) Bob Odenkirk has admitted that he had a lot of doubts over whether Better Call Saul would actually work. It was certainly a daunting task trying to make a Breaking Bad spin-off and had a lot to live up to.

(336) Saul Goodman was designed to be a somewhat anachronistic character in Breaking Bad. Saul sometimes feels like a man who has just wandered into the present day from the 1970s.

(337) The music playing in Full Measure when Mike takes out the cartel goons at the warehouse is the Beastie Boys' Shambala.

(338) Vince Gilligan said a big motivation for Walter White turning to crime is his fear of being irrelevant and then forgotten after his death. Walter would rather be a bad somebody than a good nobody.

(339) Lawson (played by Jim Beaver) is a veteran arms dealer in Albuquerque. We see Walt use his services twice in Breaking Bad and in Better Call Saul we see Lawson showing Mike some sniper rifles. Lawson is a reliable person to do business with and very professional and careful. He has some similarities with Ed Galbraith in these respects.

(340) David Costabile, who played Gale Boetticher, said it was tough work singing Major Tom (Coming Home) for Gale's karaoke performance because the song is over four minutes long. They made him do the whole song - although not all of it was used in the show. You can watch the whole thing on YouTube.

(341) Bryan Cranston said that Breaking Bad was the most exhausting acting job he has ever done.

(342) Jesse Plemons played the villain in the Black Mirror episode USS Callister. They gave Aaron Paul a voice cameo in the episode so that there was a Todd/Jesse Breaking Bad Easter egg. Aaron later took a more substantial part in the Black Mirror episode Beyond the Sea.

(343) Skinny Pete drives a 1972 Ford Thunderbird.

(344) Jesse Plemons described his character Todd as someone who is 'confusing' and hard to figure out. Todd seems like a nice young man who you'd meet at church but in reality has about the same amount of empathy and humanity as Ted Bundy.

(345) Bob Odenkirk said he had to give a completely different performance in Better Call Saul because he was essentially playing a different character. Saul and Jimmy are very different people. Saul is the worst of Jimmy but Jimmy in and of himself is a reasonably likeable person.

(346) David Costabile said he had to endlessly listen to Major Tom (Coming Home) to prepare for Gale's legendary karaoke performance. David obviously had to know the song by heart because it is supposed to be a favorite of Gale.

(347) Mike Ehrmantraut drives a 1988 Chrysler Fifth Avenue car.

(348) Laura Fraser, who played Lydia Rodarte-Quayle, said she'd never watched Breaking Bad before she was cast but had heard of the show.

(349) Aaron Paul felt that Jesse Pinkman was essentially trying to be someone that he wasn't throughout Breaking

Bad. Jesse was basically a decent person who had some potential but he somehow got dragged into this crazy meth and crime world and couldn't quite manage to climb out.

(350) The real location for Hank and Marie's house in Breaking Bad is 4901 Cumbre Del Sur Ct NE Albuquerque, NM 87111.

(351) Dean Norris was told two years in advance by Vince Gilligan that Hank was going to be killed.

(352) Eagle-eyed fans will have probably noticed that Chuck McGill (in Better Call Saul) lives in the same street as Jesse Pinkman did in most of Breaking Bad. It seems unlikely though that their paths ever crossed - unless it was in court!

(353) Bryan Cranston studied police science as a student. However, he obviously decided that he didn't want to go into law enforcement as a career.

(354) When he has to go into hiding, Saul Goodman/Jimmy ends up working in a Cinnabon branch manager in a mall in Omaha using the name Gene Takavic. Cinnabon is a real company which began in 1985. Jimmy finds this job somewhat wearing and dull to say the least but it is necessary because he needs a mundane ordinary legit cover life to stay off the radar and not attract any attention. Presumably, Jimmy was planning to move on at some point when it was safe.

(355) Vince Gilligan said that he genuinely didn't have a clue where the story in Breaking Bad was going to go when he first started writing it. It was something they figured out season by season.

(356) The finale of Breaking Bad was a huge boost for Netflix because mentions of the streaming site on social media reached an all time high for the time.

(357) Jesse was supposed to be killed off in the first season but they changed their minds about this because of the chemistry between Aaron Paul and Bryan Cranston.

(358) The make-up effects for Gus Fring's memorable death were done by the team on AMC's other big show at the time - The Walking Dead.

(359) A poll for the survey site YouGov found that 86% of people had heard of Breaking Bad. Of those familiar with the show only 9% had a negative opinion.

(360) Peter Schuler is the CEO of Madrigal Electromotive conglomerate's food-services subsidiary. Schuler has a close (and criminal) bond with Gus Fring. A memorable scene in Breaking Bad has Schuler eating tator tots to test some new dips. Tater tots are small, cylindrical pieces of deep-fried, grated potatoes. They are a popular side dish or snack in many parts of the world, especially in the United States. Tater tots are crispy on the outside and soft on the inside, and are often seasoned with salt or other spices

(361) Reid Scott auditioned to play Jesse Pinkman. Scott later appeared in Veep and the film Venom.

(362) Vince Galligan said he wrote El Camino: A Breaking Bad Movie because the question of what happened to Jesse Pinkman was the biggest loose end from Breaking Bad. We see Jesse driving away at the end of Breaking Bad but we didn't see where he went or if he even

managed to escape from the cops arriving on the scene.

(363) It is heavily implied in Better Call Saul that Mike Ehrmantraut served in the Vietnam War.

(364) The producer Christina Wayne initially felt that Aaron Paul was too handsome and clean cut to play a meth addict in Breaking Bad. She evidently came around to his casting in the end.

(365) When they were casting Breaking Bad, Bryan Cranston arranged for his interview to be pushed forward so that he could (hopefully) make a good impression before too many actors had been seen for the role. This tactic clearly did him no harm because he got the part.

(366) The United States Congress passed an act in 2005 which meant pharmacies and stores had to keep records on sales of products containing pseudoephedrine and also limit how much pseudoephedrine (in related products) one person could purchase. This was all obviously designed to make life harder for methamphetamine criminals.

(367) When he is (miserably) living as Gene in Omaha in Better Call Saul, the drink that Saul/Jimmy/Gene fixes himself whenever he gets home from the mall is a Rusty Nail. A Rusty Nail is a cocktail of Scotch, Drambuie, and lemon juice.

(368) Peter Gould was a writer, director, and producer on Breaking Bad and Better Call Saul. He was actually in charge of Better Call Saul on his own in the end.

(369) Vince Gilligan said he was very taken with the clouds in Albuquerque and they became like an extra

character in the show. They were a great tool to convey moods.

(370) Bob Odenkirk said that Saul Goodman's superpower is that he never quits or gives up.

(371) Vince Gilligan said they briefly floated the idea of Hank helping Walter in Breaking Bad after his Heisenberg secret was revealed but this idea was rejected very quickly because a 'straight arrow' like Hank would never have done that.

(372) Aaron Paul said that on Breaking Bad he would run through his lines with Bryan Cranston while they were in the makeup trailer.

(373) Mark Margolis said that even after appearing in Scarface in the early 1980s, acting still wasn't paying the bills and he had to take a temporary job in real estate to put food on the table.

(374) Meth is called Pervitin in the Czech Republic and a bigger problem than heroin. We see Lydia in Breaking Bad tell Walter White that there would be a huge market in the Czech Republic for his Blue Sky meth.

(375) Gus Fring actually appeared in more episodes of Better Call Saul than Breaking Bad.

(376) Breaking Bad aired from January 20, 2008, to September 29, 2013.

(377) In the first pilot script for Breaking Bad, Walt's car wash boss is named Amir and from Iran.

(378) The Eagle Pass Port of Entry is a border crossing

located in Eagle Pass, Texas, on the border with Mexico. Early in 2024 it was reported that Eagle Pass customs officials had seized six and a half tons of methamphetamine valued at more than $117 million. It was the biggest single meth bust the port had ever experienced.

(379) Gretchen and Elliott Schwartz are being interviewed by Charlie Rose when they appear on television near the end of Breaking Bad. Charlie Rose is an American television personality and journalist. He hosted his own talk show on PBS for many years. In 2017, he was fired from multiple positions after allegations of sexual harassment.

(380) Granite State is the nickname of New Hampshire - the state where Walter goes into hiding.

(381) A poll by the Condorcet Internet Voting Service had Jesse Pinkman ranked as the 'favorite' character in Breaking Bad.

(382) Voters on the Ranker website have Jesse Pinkman as the best Breaking Bad character. Walter White is actually third. Saul Goodman was in second place.

(383) Don Eladio Vuente tells Gus that he is 'not in Chile anymore' after the murder of Max. This implies that Gus was once someone of power and importance in Chile.

(384) There are 28 deaths in season four of Breaking Bad.

(385) The film director Darren Aronofsky was a big fan of Breaking Bad and said he was in mourning when it ended.

(386) The pop star Rihanna was famously a big fan of Breaking Bad. Aaron Paul has told some amusing anecdotes on chat shows about how she was desperate to meet him because she loved the character Jesse Pinkman.

(387) Vince Gillgan said that he was once in a restaurant and the actor Kurt Russell came over to say what a big fan of Breaking Bad he was.

(388) The Pontiac Aztek, which Walter drives in the early episodes, was seen as a naff sort of car but became cool thanks to Breaking Bad.

(389) The episode Dead Freight famously has a train heist. Jonathan Banks was previously in a train heist film as he was in Under Siege 2.

(390) Jesse Pinkman appears to own an Xbox 360.

(391) A (comic) bonus DVD feature had the whole of Breaking Bad revealed as a dream that Bryan Cranston's character Hal from Malcom in the Middle had.

(392) The El Camino is a classic American car that was produced by Chevrolet from 1959 to 1987.

(393) A real life meth dealer from Alabama named Walter White made headlines in 2013 for saying he had the best meth in the state. Apparently it was just a coincidence that he had the same name.

(394) Bob Odenkirk said the part of Saul Goodman was a godsend for him because he felt his career wasn't in a great place at the time.

(395) The Bulgarian title of Breaking Bad translates as In

the Shoes of Satan.

(396) Dean Norris said that when he auditioned to play Hank in Breaking Bad he thought the show was a comedy.

(397) The average purity of real meth smuggled into the United States prior to Breaking Bad was 37%. It later increased to 88%.

(398) Breaking Bad received 58 Emmy nominations during its run, winning 16 awards.

(399) Jesse Pinkman's blood is A negative.

(400) Krazy-8 was actually the first person that Walter told about his cancer diagnosis.

(401) The robot vacuum Jesse has in Breaking Bad is a Roomba. Roomba is a brand of robotic vacuum cleaners manufactured by iRobot. These devices are designed to autonomously clean floors in homes and businesses by navigating obstacles and following a predetermined cleaning path.

(402) The real shooting location for Jack Welker's compound was Daniel Rd NW, Albuquerque.

(403) Neil Kandy, the owner of Kandy Welding Co., is the main antagonist of El Camino. This character did not appear in Breaking Bad or Better Calll Saul but a flashback in El Camino shows us that he supplied the equipment which caged and shackled Jesse at Jack's compound.

(404) Walter White's lecture in school in Pilot about matter and how electrons and molecules change is a

parallel to how his own life will soon enter a constant (and dangerous) state of flux.

(405) Marie Schrader works as a radiologic technologist at Kleinman Radiology Center.

(406) In the scene where Jane Margolis chokes on her vomit, Krysten Ritter mostly had oatmeal in her mouth to depict this.

(407) Walter White, especially with his hair and beard in season five, looks uncannily like Gordon Freeman from Half-Life. Half-Life is a classic first-person shooter video game developed by Valve Corporation and released in 1998. It follows the story of Gordon Freeman, a scientist who must fight his way through a secret research facility after a scientific experiment goes wrong, causing a dimensional rift and unleashing alien creatures on Earth.

(408) Giancarlo Esposito turned down the part of Gus Fring initially because he was only offered a seven episode contract. He wanted a more 'intrinsic' part in the show.

(409) A lot of actors hate watching themselves and say they have never actually watched the productions they were in. This is not the case with Bryan Cranston though. Bryan said he watched every episode of Breaking Bad.

(410) Vince Gillgan said that they did the spin-off show about Saul Goodman because almost as soon as the character appeared in Breaking Bad they thought he would be a great character to do a show about. Vince said that a spin-off show about the origins of Gus Fring would have been interesting to do also.

(411) Matt Jones, who played Badger, said he got more money for one commercial than he did for his entire role in Breaking Bad.

(412) Aaron Paul spent some time with real meth addicts to prepare for playing Jesse Pinkman. Aaron said it taught him that meth is a terrible drug.

(413) Walter White's cameo in El Camino takes place in the aftermath of Walt and Jesse getting stranded in the desert in 4 Days Out.

(414) Jack Welker's primary weapon in season five is a Browning Hi-Power handgun.

(415) Jane Margolis is a tattoo artist but doesn't have any tatoos.

(416) Walter purchases a Ruger LCR in season four. The Ruger LCR is a lightweight, compact revolver.

(417) When he goes to Los Pollos Hermanos with Walt Jr, you can see Hank holding his soda cup at the top so that he can get a sample of Gus Fring's fingerprints.

(418) Caballo sin Nombre is Spanish for A Horse With No Name.

(419) Walter White's full name is Walter Hartwell White Sr.

(420) Dos Hombres Espadin is a mezcal brand created by Aaron Paul and Bryan Cranston. Mezcal is a distilled alcoholic beverage made from agave plants, primarily in Mexico. It is often compared to tequila, but has a smokier flavor. The reviews for the drink online seem a trifle

mixed.

(421) The Los Pollos Hermanos branch in Albuquerque is the 'flagship' of the chain - which explains why Gus bases himself there. Of course the real reason he's there is that Albuquerque is the home of his secret drug empire.

(422) You can, should you wish, buy a "I am the one who knocks" Breaking Bad phone case.

(423) In the spin-off show Better Call Saul, we see that Gus Fring has a secret underground passage below his house which connects to the residence next door.

(424) There has been a Breaking Bad themed slot machine in Las Vegas.

(425) Ed Galbraith has an obvious parallel to Gus Fring in that he uses a legitimate business to hide his criminal activities.

(426) Aaron Paul suffered a concussion shooting a scene where Tuco roughs up Jesse in the desert cabin.

(427) The hooker Wendy seems to have a love of Mug Root Beer. Mug Root Beer is a classic American soft drink known for its creamy and smooth flavor. It is produced by PepsiCo.

(428) Methamphetamine does not have a consistent appearance on the street because the way it is made varies. It can look like a powder or appear like little rocks.

(429) When the show ended, Aaron Paul took home the license plate from Jesse Pinkman's first car.

(430) The gun Walter has in the first ever episode is a Smith & Wesson 4506-1. He takes this gun from Krazy-8.

(431) Walter White themed graffiti has been seen in many countries around the world.

(432) Vince Gilligan said he would love there to be a Breaking Bad video game in the style of the Grand Theft Auto franchise.

(433) Bryan Cranston's first acting credit was in 1980. He appeared in a number of famous 1980s television shows like Hill Street Blues, Airwolf, Baywatch, CHiPs, and Murder, She Wrote.

(434) The axe that the crazy cartel cousins carry when they go in Walter's house to kill him is an axe used by firefighters. You couldn't buy an axe like this in a store. They had a rubber prop version of the axe too for safety reasons.

(435) The strip mall used for the exterior of Saul's office in Breaking Bad is only five minutes away from the street used for Walter's house.

(436) Some of the cartel members refer to Gus as the 'chicken man'.

(437) Vince Gilligan said that Tony Soprano was a big influence on Walter White. Tony Soprano was brilliantly played by James Gandolfini.

(438) According to a news report we see, there were 167 fatalities in the plane crash caused by Donald Margolis.

(439) Giancarlo Esposito's likeness and voice was used as

the villain in the video game Far Cry 6.

(440) The desert landscapes in Breaking Bad are symbolic of the increasing detachment the characters have from 'normal' society.

(441) The famous film director Guillermo del Toro said that he liked Better Call Saul more than Breaking Bad. He loved both shows but felt that the moral downfall of Jimmy was deeper and more poignant than Walter's arc in Breaking Bad.

(442) It is slightly ambiguous if Jane Margolis truly loves Jesse or if she is a gold digger motivated by the huge amount of money he is owed.

(443) A scene was deleted in the last ever episode of Breaking Bad where Walter talks to a former student and asks if he was a good teacher.

(444) Bob Odenkirk said that on Breaking Bad he gave Saul Goodman little moments of uncertainty and vulnerability to show that Saul wasn't quite as confident as he pretended to be.

(445) Gale Boetticher makes his first appearance in the episode Sunset.

(446) Vince Gilligan said the door is not completely shut on another Breaking Bad spin-off but for now he is happy to do other things and move on.

(447) There was a fan theory that Gale Boetticher was a sex offender. This would explain why, despite clearly being a talented scientist and affable pleasant chap, he's working in secret obscurity for a criminal. It's only a fan

theory though and wasn't confirmed.

(448) In the spin-off show Better Call Saul we see Mike fill in Saul about the details he found out about Walter White. Mike tells Saul that Walter White is 'small potatoes' and he should not have any dealings with him. Saul should have taken that advice!

(449) Aaron Paul said that Jesse's stubble was a result of him struggling to grow an actual beard.

(450) Jesse was often put in yellow clothing in Breaking Bad because yellow is seen as the color of meth.

(451) A deleted scene in El Camino had Ed Galbraith finding Jesse parked outside his vacuum store the night after Jesse's shoot out at the welding yard.

(452) Abiquiú is a small village located in northern New Mexico, near the town of Española.

(453) When they were shotting Half Measures, a member of the public thought Wendy was a real prostitute and tried to solicit her!

(454) El Camino: A Breaking Bad Movie was shot under the codename Greenbrier to keep it secret.

(455) The effects of methamphetamine typically last for about 8 to 12 hours, but can vary depending on factors such as the amount consumed, the method of administration, and an individual's tolerance to the drug.

(456) At the start of Breaking Bad, Walter has an extra job as a cashier at Bogdon's car wash. However, he is often required to wash cars too. When one of the cars

turns to belong to one of his students and the student mocks him, Walt understandably feels humiliated. This moment was doubtless a salient factor in Walter's determination to take charge of his life and become a different person.

(457) Bryan Cranston is also a talented stage actor, having appeared in Broadway productions such as All the Way.

(458) Bob Odenkirk described playing Saul Goodman as the 'role of a lifetime'.

(459) El Camino: A Breaking Bad Movie has a rating of 7.3 on IMDB. This is lower than the average scores for Breaking Bad and Better Call Saul episodes.

(460) In the episode Abiquiú, Saul says he once convinced a woman he was Kevin Costner. We see this happen in the spin-off show Better Call Saul.

(461) Sam Webb, who played Drew Sharp (the kid on the motorbike in Dead Freight), said the Breaking Bad cast didn't especially like shooting the scene where Todd shoots him and even found it a bit upsetting. Sam said it didn't bother him because he was just acting!

(462) Fly is the only episode where Anna Gunn does not appear as Skylar. We do hear her voice though.

(463) After the death of Gus Fring, Walter is irritated that he has to pay Mike a cut of his money for meth distribution. This shows us that Walter, despite considering himself to be a genius, is still a bit ignorant about the mechanics of the criminal industry he works in.

(464) In season three, Hank gets a tip-off on the phone warning him that someone is about to try and kill him. We don't find out who made that call. The logical presumption is that Gus Fring got one of his men to make the call.

(465) Vince Gilligan said that the character of Walter White was a sort of experiment in that - traditionally - characters in television shows are in a form of stasis and never really change that much from beginning to end.

(466) Gale Boetticher does at least use his chemistry talents for something harmless in that he's refined a way to make perfect coffee.

(467) Saul Goodman has an actual Scale of Justice on his desk.

(468) We see in El Camino that Ed Galbraith makes Jesse pay for the 'disappearance' he bailed out on in Breaking Bad. Ed doubtless went to a lot of time and expense to prepare a new life for Jesse so you can understand why he wants compensation for that.

(469) Jesse's experience of working in the underground superlab is described as Kafkaesque in Breaking Bad. Franz Kafka was a German-speaking Bohemian writer who is considered one of the most important figures in 20th-century literature. Kafka's surreal writing often explores themes of alienation, absurdity, and the struggle for meaning in a hostile and indifferent world.

(470) A lot of Walter White's resentment comes from a sense that he has never been appreciated. Walter probably thinks he should be wealthy and an acclaimed scientist by now but instead he's teaching at high school

and struggling to pay the bills. This could be why Walter likes having Jesse around. Jesse is one of the few people who is vocal about being impressed at how clever Walter is.

(471) Walter Jr reads the book Killing Pablo in Breaking Bad. Killing Pablo is a book written by Mark Bowden which tells the story of the hunt for and eventual killing of notorious Colombian drug lord Pablo Escobar.

(472) Giancarlo Esposito was in a number of Spike Lee films earlier in his career. School Daze, Do the Right Thing, Mo' Better Blues, and Malcolm X.

(473) Vince Gilligan said he considered having Walt Jr murdered in the show. It seems that he considered killing virtually everyone at some point!

(474) Bryan Cranston directed three episodes of Breaking Bad - Seven Thirty-Seven, No Más, Blood Money.

(475) Vince Gilligan is a big fan of western movies - an influence which is plain to see in Breaking Bad.

(476) Walter White, impressively, instals the new boiler himself when he has to replace the old one at his home. I definitely wouldn't have a clue how to fit a boiler!

(477) There was a writer's room on Breaking Bad to plan each season. This process was used to decide which ideas should stay in and which ideas should be rejected.

(478) The laptop Gus has at his office has surveillance camera footage of his superlab and poultry farm (distribution HQ). He can keep an eye on everything through this laptop.

(479) The television show that Walt Jr and his friend are watching in I.F.T. is Aqua Teen Hunger Force. Aqua Teen Hunger Force is an animated television series that was part of Adult Swim, Cartoon Network's late-night programming block.

(480) Bob Odenkirk was only supposed to play Saul Goodman in three or four episodes. He ended up playing the character for thirteen years!

(481) Vince Gilligan said that Breaking Bad was very influenced by The Treasure Of The Sierra Madre. The Treasure of the Sierra Madre is a classic film released in 1948 and directed by John Huston. The film follows a group of three men who set out to search for gold in the mountains of Mexico. As they become consumed by their greed and paranoia, their relationships begin to deteriorate and they must confront their own inner demons.

(482) Aaron Paul said that the original version of El Camino was three hours long and a lot of stuff got cut out.

(483) In 2022, bronze statues of Walter White and Jesse Pinkman were unveiled at the Albuquerque Convention Centre in New Mexico.

(484) Jesse keeps a boisterous party going in his house for days in Breaking Bad in a desperate attempt to prevent himself from thinking about the bad things he has done. You'd think that the neighbors would have complained more!

(485) In 2023 it was reported that Sergey Macheret, a teacher at Purdue School of Aeronautics and Astronautics in West Lafayette, Indiana, had been arrested for dealing

methamphetamine.

(486) In the episode 4 Days Out, Walter uses his science skills to rig a makeshift battery for the RV. Those of a scientific and mechanical bent generally say that Walter's plan wouldn't actually have worked in real life.

(487) In a poll on Ranker, Todd Alquist was ranked the seventh most hated (evil) television character. The top spot went to Joffrey Baratheon from Game of Thrones.

(488) Bryan Cranston's cameo in El Camino as Walter was top secret. He was flown in and out by private jet.

(489) Mr and Mrs Pinkman have stickers representing themselves and their youngest son on the back of their car. There is no sticker for Jesse though.

(490) Matt Jones, who played Badger, said in preparation for the part he watched a lot of online videos about the meth trade and addicts. Matt said this was a bit grim to say the least.

(491) Albuquerque hosts the annual International Balloon Fiesta - which is the largest hot air balloon festival in the world.

(492) Fans sometimes debate the moment where Walter White 'broke bad' and became a villain. Vince Gilligan said this moment actually came in Pilot for him. As soon as Walter decided to cook meth he was on a very slippery slope to a bad place.

(493) In season five you see Walter roll the barrel in the desert past the pair of pants he lost in Pilot.

(494) Jesse Pinkman essentially ends up with two father figures in Breaking Bad - Walter and Mike. The difference is that Mike genuinely cares about Jesse whereas with Walter we aren't quite so sure.

(495) Bryan Cranston did the scene where Walter throws the pizza on the roof of his house in one take. Bryan said it was an extra large pizza and quite heavy to hold and throw.

(496) Bryan Cranston said he used an old fashioned straight razor to shave his head for Breaking Bad.

(497) Giancarlo Esposito said his favorite scene as Gus Fring was when Gus calmly walked out into the sniper fire at his distribution center.

(498) Krysten Ritter said that when she was on Breaking Bad she would play Nintendo games with Aaron Paul to pass the time between takes.

(499) Walter becomes very embittered about Elliott and Gretchen Schwartz and suggests they stole his research when he sold his shares and left the company he formed with Elliott. Vince Gilligan has suggested that this was all in Walt's head and Elliott never stole any of Walter's work. It seems that Walter's bitterness mainly revolves around Gretchen - who he was once very close to. Walter is probably jealous of Elliott because he ended up with both the company and Gretchen. Elliott got the life that Walter could have had but threw away. The fact that Walt lost out on millions by selling his shares is the proverbial salt in the wound.

(500) Bryan Cranston chose to make Walter's moustache early in the show deliberately wispy and sort of pathetic.

This makes the goatee he adopts as Heisenberg rather sinister by contrast.

(501) Lavandería Brillante is the industrial laundromat Gus Fring purchased to hide his meth superlab. We see in Better Call Saul that it was Mike Ehrmantraut who was in charge of the security for the construction of the lab. The real shooting location was Delta Uniform & Linen, 1617 Candelaria NE Albuquerque. This business recently closed in real life.

(502) Including El Camino, Jonathan Banks as Mike made 85 appearances in the Breaking Bad franchise.

(503) Breaking Bad takes place over the course of two years.

(504) The point of no return for Walter is the death of Jane. It is at this point that all bets are off with Walter. He is capable of anything.

(505) Marie Schrader always seems to wear purple clothes. Vince Gilligan said that each character was color coded. Marie wears purple because purple is associated with nobility. The basic subtext is that Marie is pretentious and has put herself on a pedestal.

(506) When he did his Breaking Bad audition, Jonathan Banks improvised the moment where Mike Ehrmantraut slaps a grief stricken Jesse Pinkman after Jane's death. Mike has been sent by Saul to clean up the apartment and tell Jesse what to do.

(507) AMC was launched on October 1, 1984. It was initially known as American Movie Classics and focused on airing classic movies from the 1930s to the 1970s,

including genres such as westerns, dramas, and musicals. The channel was created as a premium cable network and was originally owned by Warner-Amex Satellite Entertainment. In the early years, AMC featured commercial-free films and also aired original programming, such as documentaries about classic films and interviews with actors and directors. The channel slowly gained a loyal viewership and became known for its high-quality film selection. In 2002, AMC underwent a rebranding to focus more on contemporary films and television series, such as Mad Men and Breaking Bad.

This shift in programming helped the channel attract a younger audience and increased its popularity among viewers. In more recent years AMC had its biggest commercial hit with The Walking Dead. Although the popularity of The Walking Dead waned in the end AMC seem determined to keep it going forever with endless spin-off shows.

(508) According to the Substance Abuse and Mental Health Services Administration (SAMHSA), about one and a half million people in the United States say they have recently taken methamphetamine.

(509) The highlighted Br and Ba in the Breaking Bad title sequence is a reference to Bromine and Barium.

(510) Krazy-8's real name is Domingo Gallardo Molina. We see in Better Call Saul that it was Lalo who gave him his nickname.

(511) Jack and Kenny liken Todd's train stunt to something from the Burt Reynolds film Hooper. Hooper is a 1978 action comedy film directed by Hal Needham, starring Burt Reynolds as the title character, a veteran

stuntman who takes on dangerous and exciting challenges to prove he still has what it takes in the world of stunt work

(512) Hank has a box-set for the acclaimed HBO series Deadwood in his house. Anna Gunn was in this show.

(513) In 2021 the BBC polled television critics from 43 countries to do a list of the greatest shows of the 21st century. Breaking Bad came in third place. The Wire and Mad Men took the top two slots.

(514) Gale is singing Tom Lehrer's "The Elements" in his lab when we meet him in Better Call Saul. "There's antimony, arsenic, aluminum, selenium, And hydrogen and oxygen and nitrogen and rhenium, And nickel, neodymium, neptunium, germanium, And iron, americium, ruthenium, uranium, Europium, zirconium, lutetium, vanadium, And lanthanum and osmium and astatine and radium..." And so on!

(515) For their 25th anniversary, the website Rotten Tomatoes conducted a poll asking people to vote for their favorite television show of the last 25 years. Breaking Bad came in first place - beating the likes of The Sopranos, Game of Thrones, and Stranger Things.

(516) Gale Boetticher has a copy of Everything's Eventual by Stephen King in his apartment. This is a short story collection.

(517) Bob Odenkirk suffered a near fatal heart attack while shooting the last season of Better Call Saul.

(518) Vince Galligan said that Breaking Bad deliberately didn't try to cast 'big name' actors so it would feel more

realistic but he would have made an exception for Clint Eastwood. You could imagine Clint Eastwood playing Ed Galbraith - although Robert Forster was absolutely perfect for that part and would have been hard to beat.

(519) It was planned that we would meet Skylar and Marie's father in season one and he was going to be played by Kris Kristofferson. In the end they decided to cancel this plan because they didn't want to stray from the main focus of the story.

(520) John de Lancie, who played Donald Margolis in Breaking Bad, is best known for his role as Q in the Star Trek franchise.

(521) Todd Alquist never seems to be aware of the gravity of murder. When he shoots the kid Drew Sharp, Todd acts as if it was no big deal at all and was clearly completely unaffected by what he had done. This gives Todd serial killer vibes. He has a lump of coal where the heart should be.

(522) Methamphetamine accounts for around 25% of drug overdoses in the United States.

(523) Gus Fring is the classic example of what is known as hiding in plain sight. He was even friends with the local DEA chief.

(524) Walt Jr is a big fan of pancakes.

(525) Laura Fraser said she pretended she could speak German when she was trying to get the part of Lydia!

(526) Walter had decided to let Krazy-8 go - until that is he noticed the missing shard of the plate he dropped (due

to passing out from a coughing fit) and realized that Krazy-8 planned to kill him with it. In this moment Walter's naive assessment of the situation is proven to be hopelessly that - naive. Walter must now make a big adjustment if he is going to continue down this path. He is going to have to be as unemotional as the criminals he know has to deal with.

(527) Bryan Cranston chose very neutral and bland clothes for Walter early on to express this very vanilla sort of character. A man who has gone through life under the radar and is secretly quite bitter about this.

(528) Jane has a mural of a falling pink teddy bear. It is later her distraught father who will cause a teddy bear to end up in Walter's pool.

(529) Victor is a henchman of Gus Fring. Gus kills him with a box-cutter in season five in what is a rare display of violence by Gus. The reason why Gus killed Victor is that Victor was seen near Gale's apartment. Gus also wanted to intimidate Walter White.

(530) Walter White, despite everything, is a strangely relatable character in Breaking Bad because he is a man who feels as if he didn't get a fair shake in life. He lost Gretchen, he lost the company he formed, he doesn't make much money as a teacher and his students mostly find his classes boring, his son has cerebral palsy, and now he has cancer. Most of us, like Walter, have felt at some point that life isn't treating us very fairly. We obviously don't become meth producers and criminals (!) or condone that but we can at least understand Walt's frustration.

(531) Jesse is a big fan of pineapple. Only 'assholes' don't

like pineapple according to Jesse. Walter on the other hand can take it or leave it.

(532) Vince Gilligan said he toyed with the idea of having Walt Jr appear in El Camino but decided against this in the end because he wanted the focus to be on Jesse and people from Jesse's life.

(533) Michael Bowen and Jesse Plemons came up with a (unseen) history for Jack and Todd. The general gist is that Jack sort of adopted Todd because Jack's sister kept getting violent boyfriends who were abusive to Todd. This would explain the close bond between Jack and Todd and the loyalty Todd has for his uncle. We can probably assume too that Jack meted out some violent justice to these abusive men. They are probably buried in the desert!

(534) Walter White's blue meth is said to be three times stronger than average street meth.

(535) Jesse's mother is called Diane. We only learned Mrs Pinkman's first name in El Camino.

(536) The cast wore black armbands on the set when Jonathan Banks shot his last scene as Mike.

(537) As a libertarian, Gale Boetticher doesn't believe that drugs should be illegal. Gale's argument is that it is better for a skilled chemist like him to be making meth than someone on the street who doesn't know what they are doing because this way the drug will be safer. While that reasoning does have some twisted logic it is unavoidable all the same that lives will be ruined and lost from the 'superior' product that Gale helps to produce. Gale would probably see himself as the lesser of two evils. If he didn't

make meth then someone else would.

(538) Giancarlo Esposito said that when his time on Breaking Bad came to an end he took a Los Pollos Hermanos cup home as a momento.

(539) Bryan Cranston started his career as a stand-up comedian. Thankfully though he turned his hand to acting.

(540) Aaron Paul said one of his favorite scenes in Breaking Bad is that awkward scene when Jesse has dinner with Walter and Skylar.

(541) Jesse Pinkman's tattoo in Breaking Bad was obviously fake. Aaron Paul said it only took ten minutes for the make-up team to put it on.

(542) Matt Jones, who played Badger, said his favorite Breaking Bad episode was the one called Better Call Saul because Badger got a memorable nine page scene at the start.

(543) Albuquerque enjoyed something of a tourism boom in the later stages of Breaking Bad.

(544) You might notice in Breaking Bad that Jesse's house seems to look different at some point. This is because the people who owned the original house used for shooting sold it and it couldn't be used anymore. They later got it back as a shooting location though.

(545) When they lost the use of the house location for Jesse what they did was try to disguise this by recreating the interior and having the outside view blocked off with a vehicle.

(546) The hooker Wendy made no appearances in Breaking Bad after season three.

(547) There is definitely something a bit Jekyll and Hyde about the way that Walter juggles Walter White and Heisenberg early on. In the end though the line becomes so blurred it is as if Walter White was never real. Jekyll and Hyde is a classic novel written by Robert Louis Stevenson, first published in 1886. The novel explores the duality of human nature and - much like Breaking Bad - the consequences of giving in to one's darker impulses.

(548) Different locations were used for Joe's Salvage yard in Breaking Bad. The main one was a metal recycling facility called Ace Metals at 5711 Broadway Boulevard Southeast, Albuquerque.

(549) To'hajiilee Reservation was the most important location used for the desert scenes in the show. To'hajiilee Reservation is a Native American reservation located in New Mexico. It is home to the To'hajiilee (Navajo) tribe and covers an area of approximately 140 square miles.

(550) Walter White makes $80 million from his involvement in the meth business. He obviously has a lot less than this by the end though.

(551) Bryan Cranston said that one of his favorite moments in Breaking Bad was the musical montage of the hooker Wendy going about her grim daily trade.

(552) Jimmy McGill has an office at the back of a Vietnamese nail salon in Better Call Saul. The salon doesn't always look identical - which obviously suggests more than one location was used.

(553) Methamphetamine is sometimes called 'redneck cocaine' on the street.

(554) Breaking Bad arose from Vince Gilligan and a friend joking that they might have to resort to making meth in an RV to earn a living.

(555) The final fate of Gus Fring rather evokes the Batman villain Two-Face.

(556) The 'Blue Sky' meth made by Walter White makes a cameo in AMC's The Walking Dead. In that show you see some blue meth in Merle Dixon's drug stash. Merle was the brother of Daryl Dixon.

(557) Aaron Paul said that when he wrapped his last ever scene on Breaking Bad he had to go straight to the airport to go and do another acting job. He said he was in a state of mourning and it felt surreal to think that Breaking Bad was over.

(558) In the episode Cat's in the Bag, we see Jesse watching The Three Stooges on television.

(559) In the episode Cancer Man, we see Walt Jr watching the film Earth vs. the Flying Saucers. Earth vs. the Flying Saucers is a 1956 science fiction film directed by Fred F. Sears. The film follows a scientist who must work with the military to stop (as the title of the film implies!) an alien invasion of Earth by flying saucers.

(560) What makes Tuco a compelling villain is that he is dangerously unpredictable. He can have moments of calm where it seems like he's being reasonable but in a split second he'll suddenly snap and do something violent without provocation.

(561) It is noticeable that Gus Fring, who owns a fast food franchise, serves much healthier fruit and vegetable platters at his business meetings.

(562) The Better Call Saul episode titled Magic Man was dedicated to Robert Forster - who had recently passed away.

(563) Walter wears a porkpie hat when he transforms into Heisenberg. The hat's name was originally derived from its resemblance to the Melton Mowbray pork pie - a famous pastry originating from the market town of Melton Mowbray in England around the 1760s

(564) Hector Salamanca obviously has a knowledge of Morse code because he uses it on his wheelchair bell. Morse code is a method of encoding text characters using a series of dots and dashes. Each letter in the alphabet is represented by a unique combination of dots and dashes, and spaces are used to separate words. This code was commonly used for long-distance communication before the advent of telephones and other modern forms of communication.

(565) There are a couple of rare occasions in the show where Jesse calls Walter by the name 'Walt'. The vast majority of the time though Jesse calls him Mr White.

(566) Bryan Cranston took home Heisenberg's hat and sunglasses when the show ended.

(567) Vince Gilligan said he chose the name 'White' because it is 'vanilla and bland'.

(568) Wilshire Community Police Station in Los Angeles was used for some exterior shots in Breaking Bad. This

was a rare instance of an exterior outside New Mexico being used.

(569) Jesse and Jane have an interest in superhero art. Krysten Ritter would later play the Marvel superhero Jessica Jones.

(570) The episode title No Más means 'no more' in Spanish. No Más was what the boxer Roberto Duran famously said to the referee when he quit in his rematch with Sugar Ray Leonard. Duran had become frustrated by Leonard's clowning and mockery of him in the ring.

(571) Albuquerque experiences over 300 days of sunshine per year, making it one of the sunniest cities in the United States.

(572) Daniel Wormald is a character who features in Better Call Saul. This is the nerdy man who hires Mike to protect him when he does deals with Nacho. Daniel is mentioned but unseen in Breaking Bad. He owns Lazer Base - the laser tag place that Saul uses for money laundering and wants Walt and Skylar to buy. As Saul explains, when it comes to money laundering, you need a 'Danny'.

(573) Famous people who were born in Albuquerque include Neil Patrick Harris, Jeff Bezos, and Demi Lovato.

(574) Ed Gailbraith's store is called Best Quality Vacuum.

(575) In the episode ABQ, Hank says "Anyone, anyone, Bueller?" This is obviously a reference to the boring teacher in the cultish John Hughes film Ferris Bueller's Day Off.

(576) Near the end of Breaking Bad, Saul is told by his secretary that Danny's Lazer Base has been seized by the DEA. The authorities are basically choking off Saul's connections and income as the net tightens. He has no choice but to go into hiding.

(577) Mike tells Walter in Breaking Bad that just because you shoot Jesse James that doesn't make you Jesse James. Jesse James was an American outlaw, bank and train robber, guerrilla, and the leader of the James-Younger Gang. He was born in 1847 and became one of the most notorious and infamous outlaws of the American Old West. James and his gang were responsible for numerous robberies and murders, and his exploits made him a legendary figure in American history. He was eventually shot and killed by fellow gang member Robert Ford in 1882.

(578) Ice Station Zebra Associates is the name of the company Saul Goodman uses for tax evasion. Ice Station Zebra is a novel written by Alistair MacLean in 1963. The story is set in the Cold War era and follows a British spy who is sent to a remote Arctic weather station called Ice Station Zebra. The spy must navigate through treacherous conditions and face off against enemies in order to retrieve important information that could affect global politics. The novel was also adapted into a film in 1968 starring Rock Hudson and Ernest Borgnine.

(579) It is probable that Gus Fring's chicken franchise alone has already made him a millionaire. However, Los Pollos Hermanos is small change compared to Gus Fring's drugs empire. Gus is merely using Los Pollos Hermanos as a front from which to make a much bigger fortune.

(580) Walter obviously wouldn't have been able to throw the pizza on the roof of his house if it was sliced. To this end, a later scene has Badger telling Jesse that the place he got pizzas from doesn't slice them.

(581) You can see Krysten Ritter breathing when Mike comes in to clean the room after Jane's death.

(582) At 5314 feet above sea level, Albuquerque is the highest metropolitan city in America.

(583) The plot of the episode 4 Days Out is inspired by the film The Flight of the Phoenix. The Flight of the Phoenix is a 1965 American survival drama film directed by Robert Aldrich, based on the 1964 novel The Flight of the Phoenix by Elleston Trevor. It stars James Stewart, Richard Attenborough, Peter Finch, and Hardy Krüger. The film follows the story of a group of men stranded in the Sahara desert after their plane crashes. As they struggle to survive in the harsh environment, they come up with a daring plan to build a new plane out of the wreckage in order to escape.

(584) One could interpret parallels between meat/fast food and meth when it comes to Gus Fring in Breaking Bad. In both his public and secret life he is peddling something which isn't very good for people. Both the meat industry and the meth trade are grim affairs to say the least. Gus doesn't care about any of this though. It is all about profit.

(585) Bob Odenkirk said he wasn't that familiar with Breaking Bad when he was offered the part of Saul Goodman but he was swayed by his agent - who told him that Breaking Bad was the sort of show that won Emmy awards.

(586) Walter White's mother is mentioned in Breaking Break (Walt pretends to go and see her at one point) but we don't actually meet her and she remains an unseen character.

(587) Albuquerque was founded in 1706 as a Spanish colonial outpost and was later incorporated as a city in 1885.

(588) Jesse's parents made their last appearance in Caballo Sin Nombre - though they did return for the film El Camino. Jesse and his parents were never on exactly great terms but Jesse using Saul Goodman to make them sell him his aunt's house at a knock down price was probably the final straw. Not to say Jesse's parents were not very sympathetic characters. They basically made their son homeless!

(589) When he first moves out of the family home, Walter's new residence has the number 221. This is the same house number as Sherlock Holmes.

(590) Breaking Bad examines the ways in which individuals justify or rationalize their actions, especially when they are morally ambiguous or clearly wrong. Walter knows that what he is doing is wrong but he tries to convince himself he is doing it for others - thus deluding himself.

(591) The Candy Lady, a store in Albuquerque, made the blue candy which was used for the meth Walter and Jesse make. Aaron Paul said he ate quite a bit of this blue candy making Breaking Bad.

(592) Jesse is seen to hallucinate at one point from taking meth. Meth users have said this scene is not accurate

because meth doesn't have that effect. However, sleep deprivation from taking meth CAN have a similar effect.

(593) Hank tells Jack his name is ASAC Hank Schrader. ASAC means Assistant Special Agent in Charge of the DEA.

(594) Zafiro Añejo is the fictional tequila in Breaking Bad and Better Call Saul. Zafiro means sapphire and Añejo means vintage.

(595) A possible plot hole is that Jack and the neo-Nazis get $70 million of Walter's money but then continue living in a dusty compound making meth AND with Jesse as a captive slave. Why are they carry on as normal now that they are rich? We can probably presume that they don't know anything else and are well aware that if they suddenly started buying mansions and sports cars they would look suspicious. It seems likely they have started laundering the money. We also see in El Camino that Todd had a large amount of cash hidden in his fridge.

(596) Peter Schuler of Madrigal Electromotive is clearly as thick as thieves with Gus Fring and been a great help to his meth empire. However, the exact nature of this criminal business partnership is left a bit on the vague side. It is up to us to fill in some of the blanks for ourselves.

(597) Ed Galbraith's position as the boss of a vacuum cleaner repair/sales shop isn't just a fake cover. El Camino shows that he really DOES spend most of his time doing this.

(598) The writers on Breaking Bad said they never quite decided if Ted Beneke was blackmailing Skylar. It seems

logical to presume that he was because he must have known that Skylar (and Walt) would be audited if he went down.

(599) The shooting location for where the hooker Wendy plies her trade in the early seasons was the Crossroads Motel, 001 Central Ave NE, Albuquerque.

(600) Aaron Paul's Breaking Bad tattoo says 'No half measures' - a famous line from the show.

(601) The Drug Enforcement Administration (DEA) was established on July 1, 1973, by President Richard Nixon in response to the increasing drug abuse problem in the United States. It was created by merging the Bureau of Narcotics and Dangerous Drugs (BNDD) and the Office of Drug Abuse Law Enforcement (ODALE) to create a single, unified agency to enforce federal drug laws.

(602) The scenes in Breaking Bad at Don Eladio's swimming pool were shot in Placitas, New Mexico.

(603) Aaron Paul was once a contestant on The Price is Right. The Price is Right is a popular game show where contestants compete to win cash and prizes by guessing the price of merchandise. The show first premiered in 1956 and has since become a staple of daytime television.

(604) There was a cartoon called Better Call Saul Presents: Slippin' Jimmy in 2022. The cartoon was about a young Saul/Jimmy. It only lasted six episodes and got atrocious reviews.

(605) After he gets his house back (thanks to some chicanery from Saul) in Breaking Bad, Saul tells Jesse that he is now 'house poor'. This is obviously a real

phenomenon. Jesse owns a house but now doesn't have any money because it all went into buying the house.

(606) Bryan Cranston said his research for Breaking Bad once led him to detect the presence of a meth lab in the area where he lived. It was the smell which alerted him.

(607) Over the course of the show, an average of just over four people die in the span of each episode. The plane crash obviously exaggerates these figures somewhat.

(608) The train sequence in Dead Freight was tough to shoot. Some digital effects were used to depict Todd's exploits.

(609) We didn't see it happen in the show but Vince Gilligan suggested that Walter poisoned Brock via a juice box at school.

(610) One of Pontiac Aztek cars used in the show sold for over $7,000 online when the series ended.

(611) President Obama was a big fan of Breaking Bad. He actually invited Bryan Cranston to the White House.

(612) There are 15 deaths in season 5A of Breaking Bad.

(613) There are 23 deaths in season 5B of Breaking Bad.

(614) George Merkert (played by Michael Shamus Wiles) is the Assistant Special Agent in Charge (ASAC) of the Albuquerque DEA Field Office. He is Hank's boss in the show. Merket is forced out of the DEA in the end because he was good friends with Gus Fring but failed to deduce that Gus was a major criminal with a substantial meth empire and cartel connections.

(615) Walt declines Saul Goodman's proposal to launder his money through a laser tag business. This has a nice irony later on when Walt uses Badger and Pete to spook Elliott and Gretchen with lasers - and thus get them to agree to take Walt's money to give to Walt Jr.

(616) Breaking Bad has the local DEA offices central to the city in a fairly busy spot. In reality the DEA office in Albuquerque is a bit more out of town.

(617) In the original pilot script for Breaking Bad, Walt crashes the RV in a field where cows are grazing. This original pilot was set in California.

(618) In the spin-off Better Call Saul, we see that Jimmy's brother Chuck often wears a space blanket at home to protect himself from anything electrical. A space blanket, also known as a mylar blanket or emergency blanket, is a lightweight, reflective blanket that is designed to retain and reflect body heat. It is often used in emergency situations.

(619) Ed Galbraith charges $125,000 in cash for the "deluxe" service. If you have this amount in cash he will give you a new identity.

(620) Jesse goes to Alaska in El Camino. In a flashback we see it was Mike who suggested Alaska.

(621) Mark Margolis said that when he played Hector Salamanca he drew on his own experiences with his mother in law - who was left unable to speak after a stroke.

(622) Vince Gilligan said in an interview with the BBC that the fame of Breaking Bad was unavoidably helped by

piracy and illegal streams - which meant more people were able to watch it. Vince obviously wasn't condoning piracy but just pointing out an obvious fact.

(623) An article in The Guardian in 2013 reported that Jeffrey Katzenberg, head of Dreamworks Studio, was offering to pay $75 million for three new Breaking Bad short films which would become content for mobile telephones. Needless to say, this ambitious idea never came to pass.

(624) A man named Ryan Lee Carroll from Florida won a competition to watch the Breaking Bad finale at a private party with the cast. A year later he was charged with possessing drugs. The police refused to say if one of them was meth.

(625) Bryan Cranston said that he thought the train heist was the best sequence in Breaking Bad because you had the 'fun' and excitement of the heist but then were brought crashing back down to earth when Todd shot the kid on the bike. Bryan felt this moment was powerful and necessary because it reminded us that crime is not a 'caper' but a horrible and ruthless business.

(626) We don't actually see if Gus Fring really does have a family in Breaking Bad. This is something that saddened Giancarlo Esposito because he wanted scenes where we see Gus with his children at home, posing as the nice family man.

(627) El Camino was shown in select theaters across the United States. Most people obviously watched it on Netflix though.

(628) In an interview in 2015, the actor and comedian

Billy Crystal said he binged the whole of Breaking Bad in six days!

(629) Some local actors were cast in Breaking Bad so that the make-up of Albuquerque was represented in the show. Steven Michael Quezada for example, who played Steve Gomez, is from Albuquerque.

(630) They did a nationwide search to find an actor with cerebral palsy to play Walt Jr.

(631) Vince Gilligan said the reason why Breaking Bad was originally set in California is that he lived there and liked the idea of going home to his house each night after shooting!

(632) Jesse Pinkman's fashion style has been described as skater boy/hip hop.

(633) Jonathan Banks said he would sometimes disagree with the writers on something they had Mike say or do but ultimately he would defer to them because it was their show and they knew what they were doing.

(634) In the scene where Saul gets Jesse his house back at a bargain price by threatening to reveal that meth was cooked there, you can see that Saul has some contempt for the pompous lawyer representing Mr and Mrs Pinkman. This is very in sync with what we later see in Better Call Saul. Jimmy just isn't cut out for the mainstream legal world and hates the self-importance of the lawyers who operate there. What grinds Jimmy's gears more than anything is that the lawyers from that world never saw him as an equal or peer - especially his brother Chuck.

(635) Vince Gilligan said the character who changed the most from his original conception was Hank. He credited Dean Norris with Hank becoming more complex than the original broad brush for the character.

(636) According to drug information websites, meth addicts can build up an increasing tolerance to the drug. This means that the 'high' is never as good again as their early experiences.

(637) You can buy a number of Breaking Bad jigsaw puzzles.

(638) The thing which appealed to AMC about Breaking Bad was that it was a modern crime show. They had just commissioned the period show Mad Men and were still primarily known for showing old movies so Breaking Bad was a good way to show there was more to AMC than period shows and films.

(639) Very early in the run of Breaking Bad, Bryan Cranston was nominated for an Emmy and actually won for his performance as Walter White. This was a great thrill and boost for the cast and crew because it showed them that their show, which hadn't set the world alight when it came to viewing figures, had been noticed and judged to be great drama.

(640) Walter White has to go through chemo treatments in Breaking Bad. Chemotherapy is a type of cancer treatment that uses drugs to kill cancer cells or stop them from growing and multiplying. It is most commonly used to treat cancer that has spread to other parts of the body or when surgery or radiation therapy alone is not enough to eliminate the cancer. Chemotherapy can be administered orally, intravenously, or through injection

and may be used in combination with other cancer treatments. It can have various side effects, such as nausea, fatigue, and an increased risk of infection.

(641) Before he accepted the part of Walter White, AMC sent Bryan Cranston copies of the first two episodes of Mad Men so that he could see how serious they were about making high quality drama.

(642) Dean Norris said that after shooting his last ever scene as Hank in Breaking Bad he had to hop on a plane and go to another job. He said this felt very weird.

(643) Lavell Crawford, who played Saul Goodman's bodyguard (and pickpocket) Huell Babineaux, lost 120 pounds in weight between Breaking Bad and the prequel show Better Call Saul. I suppose we have to presume that Huell put a lot of weight on over the years!

(644) Gale Boetticher is a vegan - which is apparent to the police from the food and written recipes in his apartment. This is an important detail because it makes Hank suspicious when he learns Gale had the number/details of the fast food chicken joint Los Pollos Hermanos among his possessions.

(645) AMC were allegedly interested in Matthew Broderick for the part of Walter White. Bryan Cranston was always Vince Gilligan's first choice but AMC were not initially convinced by Cranston and allegedly tried to shop the part around before they agreed to cast him. Bryan Cranston said that Matthew Broderick's name was on a list of actors who might potentially play Walter White but he wasn't actually offered the part.

(646) A mix of practical and visual effects were used for

the moment where Gus Fring emerges from Hector's room with part of his face missing.

(647) Breaking Bad did not get amazing viewing figures for most of its existence. It was only late in the show when positive word of mouth created a big buzz around the series.

(648) There are some similarities between Walter White and the real life Ross Ulbricht. Ross Ulbricht is an American man who founded and operated the dark web marketplace, Silk Road. He was arrested in 2013 and convicted in 2015 on charges of money laundering, conspiracy to commit computer hacking, conspiracy to traffic narcotics, and other offenses related to running Silk Road. Ulbricht was sentenced to life in prison without the possibility of parole. Ross Ulbricht had degrees in physics and engineering and was a former Eagle Scout who ran a second-hand book business. You could say he was a bit like Walter White in that he was an intelligent and seemingly ordinary man whose life suddenly took an unexpectedly dark twist.

(649) It is implied that Mike was a sniper in Better Call Saul as he seems to know a lot about the M40 bolt-action rifle.

(650) The interior of Walt and Jesse's RV was recreated in the studio so that it could be rocked around in scenes where it is on the move.

(651) When the show wrapped, Bryan Cranston got a Breaking Bad tattoo on his finger. Aaron Paul also got a Breaking Bad themed tattoo.

(652) The first thing that Bob Odenkirk shot for Breaking

Bad was Saul Goodman's commercial.

(653) Jonathan Banks was not happy with the way Mike fled and left town when the heat got too much in Breaking Bad. Jonathan felt that Mike would not have left without saying goodbye to his granddaughter and that he wouldn't have just left her in the park.

(654) Daniel and Luis Moncada, who played the enforcers Leonel and Marco Salamanca, really were in a gang in real life. Luis served some time in prison and said shooting guns in Breaking Bad was difficult because it gave him flashbacks to his gang days.

(655) When he works in Gus Fring's lab, Walter takes a peanut butter and jelly sandwich (with the crusts cut off) with him for lunch. This sandwich combination is generally credited to Julia Davis Chandler. In 1901, she was the first to name this type of sandwich in the Boston Cooking School Magazine of Culinary Science & Domestic Economics.

(656) Laura Fraser said her own fashion is nothing like Lydia Rodarte-Quayle because in real life she rarely wears make-up and prefers sneakers to fancy shoes.

(657) Jesse Pinkman has a Kawasaki motorcycle at the start of Breaking Bad but it gets stolen.

(658) Vince Gilligan said it is very deliberate that Breaking Bad riffs on MacGyver when Walter White has to 'science' his way out of a tricky situation. MacGyver is a television series that originally aired in the 1980s and follows the adventures of the title character, Angus MacGyver, a resourceful and clever secret agent who uses his scientific knowledge and problem-solving skills to

save the day. The show is known for its inventive and unconventional solutions to problems, with MacGyver often using everyday objects to build contraptions and escape dangerous situations. There was a modern remake of MacGyver quite recently.

(659) Jonathan Banks said the most fun he had on Breaking Bad was when Mike takes Jesse out in the desert and they have to drive all over the place together. Jonathan said there were lots of laughs shooting these scenes.

(660) Gale Boetticher was supposed to sing Breakfast in America by Supertramp in the karaoke clip that Hank finds. They had to scrap this idea because it was too expensive to get the rights.

(661) The song Major Tom (Coming Home) obviously takes some inspiration from David Bowie's Space Oddity.

(662) Bob Odenkirk said they had to make Saul (Jimmy) more likeable in the spin-off show because the Saul Goodman character from Breaking Bad would have worn out his welcome very quickly in a solo show. The character needed more nuance, depth, and a backstory.

(663) AMC planned to end Breaking Bad after the third season. FX channel, on hearing this whisper, expressed an interest in giving the show a new home for a fourth season. AMC then changed their mind and decided to continue with the show.

(664) The house that Jesse lives in at the start of Breaking Bad was owned by his late aunt - who died of cancer. Jesse clearly loved his aunt and we learn it was Jesse who helped looked after her when she was sick. The house

therefore has sentimental value to Jesse - plus of course also giving him a roof over his head. Jesse believes his aunt wanted him to have this house but his parents, as we see in the show, have other ideas.

(665) Krazy-8 was supposed to die in the first episode but he stayed around for longer because they were enjoying the performance of Maximino Arciniega.

(666) Aaron Paul was 42 when he appeared in Better Call Saul. Jesse is supposed to be in his early 20s in the scenes Aaron did.

(667) You can buy Breaking Bad fridge magnets.

(668) A popular Breaking Bad merch item is a mug with the Los Pollos Hermanos logo on it.

(669) Hector Salamanca's car (before his stroke) is a 1960 Chevrolet Impala.

(670) The country where the last ever episode of Breaking Bad was the most pirated was Australia. Australia accounted for 18% of all torrents for this episode.

(671) There was a deleted scene in El Camino which featured Skinny Pete flushing drugs down the toilet and preparing for the arrival of the police. This is after he helped Jesse flee.

(672) Laura Fraser said that when she was cast as Lydia in Breaking Bad, in order to get to speed, she binged four seasons of the show in four days.

(673) The last words of Gus Fring are - "Last chance to look at me, Hector."

(674) The Breaking Bad character Patrick Kuby was supposed to appear in Better Call Saul but couldn't in the end because the actor Bill Burr had a relative who was ill and understandably made that his priority.

(675) Laura Fraser said in an interview that she thinks Lydia's habit of putting milk in chamomile tea is revolting!

(676) We never find out what Skinny Pete's last name is.

(677) The name of the band that Jesse Pinkman used to be in is TwaüghtHammër.

(678) Adam Godley, the actor who played Elliott Schwartz, is actually English in real life.

(679) Kim Wrexler seems to be a fan of horror films in Better Call Saul. She invites Jimmy to watch The Evil Dead and John Carpenter's The Thing.

(680) One of the books in Gale Boetticher's apartment is called Fundamentals of Marxism Leninism.

(681) Gus Fring seems to be able to speak German - which is obviously useful given his connections to Madrigal.

(682) Gale Boetticher's apartment includes a picture of him on Mount Everest.

(683) We see Jimmy watching Ice Station Zebra in Better Call Saul. This is the name he uses for his tax dodge company in Breaking Bad.

(684) Despite his memorable karaoke performance as

Gale, David Costabile said the thought of doing karaoke in real life would terrify him.

(685) The episode Seven Thirty-Seven takes its title from the amount of money Walt calculates he needs to make for his family - $737,000.

(686) In season two, the homeless Jesse tries to crash with his old TwaüghtHammër bandmate Paul Tyree (Drew Waters). We see that Paul is nothing like Jesse and his friends now. He has a nice house, a son, a wife, and dresses in somewhat preppy clothes. Paul seems willing to help Jesse out but this is scuppered by Paul's wife Sara (Shauna McLean) - who plainly wants Jesse out of the house ASAP.

(687) Jonathan Banks said that Mike was sort of inspired by Max von Sydow's assassin Joubert from Three Days of the Condor. Three Days of the Condor is a 1975 political thriller film directed by Sydney Pollack and starring Robert Redford. The film follows a CIA researcher named Joe Turner (played by Redford) who works in a clandestine office in New York City. One day, Turner returns from lunch to find all of his coworkers murdered. He goes on the run, trying to stay one step ahead of the mysterious forces who are hunting him down.

(688) Skylar later replaces her 1991 Jeep Grand Wagoneer with a 2012 Ford Edge Limited.

(689) Marie never meets Saul Goodman in Breaking Bad. She does though get to confront him in Better Call Saul.

(690) Laura Fraser described Todd as a 'sick bunny' for having a crush on Lydia!

(691) In 2018, it was reported that a customer named Parker Twede in Provo, Utah, had written a letter of complaint about Blue Sky rock candy for sale. His letter of complaint was as follows - 'Hello, I was at your store in Provo, UT yesterday and was completely appalled by one of the products you carry. Let me preface by saying that I am not by any means easily-offended. When I saw the end cap full of breaking bad (sic) candy meth, I couldn't believe my eyes. What kind of example are you trying to set for the children in your store? This is beyond unacceptable and tacky. I have several family members and friends who have been affected by this horrible drug. To say this is insensitive is a giant understatement. I ask that you please remove this product from your stores as it is glorifying meth use. Shame on you.'

(692) People have printed out the Los Pollos Hermanos menus online. Despite the name of the franchise there isn't actually a huge amount of chicken on the menu.

(693) You can actually buy a Gus Fring wall calendar on Etsy.

(694) Vince Gilligan said that, even at the start of the show, it is supposed to be detectable that Walter has a suppressed antipathy towards Hank. Hank has a very important job, is promoted, and is a larger than life macho frat boy type of person who is popular and charismatic. He is everything that the meek high school teacher Walter isn't. Walter also might be jealous of the fact that Hank and Marie clearly make more money than him and Skylar. Hank's house looks more expensive than the one Walter lives in.

(695) Bryan Cranston said that until he was cast in Malcom in the Middle he hadn't actually made much

money from acting.

(696) Although the character Hank gets involved in a number of shoot outs in Breaking Bad, Dean Norris said that in his research for the role he learned that 99% of DEA officers and cops had never had to use their gun.

(697) Michael McKean, who played Chuck McGill in Better Call Saul, is best known for his memorable performance as David St Hubbins in the classic comedy film This is Spinal Tap.

(698) Walter using fulminated mercury to create an explosion in the first season was inspired by the 1955 John Ford film Mister Roberts. The film is set on a cargo ship and has a character using a similar method to create explosions.

(699) Lydia Rodarte-Quayle's name seems to be a mash-up of the fashion brand Rodarte and Dan Quayle - who served as the 44th Vice President of the United States from 1989 to 1993 under President George H. W. Bush. Quayle was known for his infamous gaffes, most notably misspelling the word "potato" as "potatoe" during a school visit in 1992. Lydia's name could be construed as a commentary on her as a person. She is stylish in appearance but not as clever as she thinks.

(700) Vince Gilligan said his one regret on Breaking Bad is that he didn't direct more episodes.

(701) The film director Steven Soderbergh is a fan of Breaking Bad. He even proposed that the last two episodes should have been shown in cinemas.

(702) Vince Gilligan said he had given up on Breaking

Bad ever being made when AMC got in touch to arrange a meeting.

(703) Breaking Bad is sometimes credited as being one of the first shows that was 'binged' due to its first three seasons dropping on Netflix while it was still in production.

(704) Even though they had worked together on an episode of The X-Files, Bryan Cranston said he didn't actually remember who Vince Gilligan was at first when he was contacted about Breaking Bad.

(705) Walter White always tried to explain his detour into crime, murder and the drug trade as something he had to do to provide financial security for his family. In the last ever episode though he admits that he did it all for himself. He enjoyed being Heisenberg and was good at it. It made him feel alive in a way he never had before.

(706) Giancarlo Esposito said that when he played Gus Fring a big inspiration to him was Edward James Olmos as Lieutenant Martin "Marty" Castillo in Miami Vice. Rather than play the usual bad tempered shouty police chief, Olmos played his character in Miami Vice in a very quiet, reserved, calculating sort of way. Esposito was actually in Miami Vice.

(707) The location used for the exterior of Saul Goodman's office was the Dale City Sports Bar in Albuquerque.

(708) Mike has a meeting in a diner with Lydia Rodarte-Quayle after the death of Gus. Mike tells Lydia to lose the oversized sunglasses because he feels 'like he's talking to Jackie Onassis'. Jacqueline Kennedy Onassis, born

Jacqueline Lee Bouvier, was the wife of President John F. Kennedy and served as First Lady of the United States from 1961 to 1963. After President Kennedy's assassination, she remarried Greek shipping magnate Aristotle Onassis and became known as Jackie Onassis. Jackie Onassis was partial to a pair of oversized sunglasses.

(709) Saul Goodman's Cadillac in Breaking Bad has LWYRUP on the plate. This means lawyer up (get a lawyer).

(710) Vince Gilligan said that Gale Boetticher, who is briefly Walter's new lab assistant, was specifically designed to be the polar opposite of Jesse Pinkman.

(711) We never see Saul Goodman at home in Breaking Bad or learn anything about his private life. This of course would all come in the spin-off show.

(712) Jesse Pinkman is a big fan of beanie hats. He sports a variety of them in Breaking Bad.

(713) Bryan Cranston said he put on some weight to play Walter White because he wanted the character to look a bit 'dumpy'. Bryan was naturally a bit horrified then when he deduced he would have to play a number of early scenes in his underwear!

(714) Charles Haid directed an episode of Breaking Bad. Haid played Officer Andy Renko in Hill Street Blues - which was arguably the greatest police television show ever made.

(715) Los Pollos Hermanos is a Madrigal corporate franchise. This arrangement is probably necessary for

Gus because he has to launder a lot of drug money and Madrigal's Peter Schuler is key to that.

(716) The episodes in season two with a flash forward have the title Seven Thirty-Seven Down Over ABQ when connected.

(717) When we first meet him, Gus Fring speaks in a deeper voice when he drops the fast food manager persona and is purely Gus Fring - drug baron. They soon stopped doing this though.

(718) The teasers for season two suggested there would an explosion at Walter's house and people there would die. This obviously didn't quite turn out to be the case though.

(719) The pink teddy bear in Breaking Bad has been refashioned 'Heisenbear' in Breaking Bad merch.

(720) You can buy Breaking Bad hoodies from the merch store.

(721) Tuco is a novelty because he is a Salamanca but it wasn't Gus Fring who had him killed!

(722) Vince Gilligan said he was relieved in one sense when Breaking Bad ended because he didn't have 'Walter White in my head anymore'.

(723) The last words Walter White says in the show are - "Well, goodbye Lydia."

(724) Hector Salamanca is rare among his family because he died by suicide rather than murder.

(725) Laura Fraser said that, unlike Lydia, she has never

actually tried Stevia in real life.

(726) We see oranges fall after Ted Beneke takes a tumble in Crawl Space. This is probably a reference to The Godfather - where oranges are used as a symbol of death.

(727) The first line that Mike Ehrmantraut has in Breaking Bad is - "Saul Goodman sent me."

(728) The last time we see Huell Babineaux in Breaking Bad he's sitting in a DEA safehouse. Fans have joked that he's probably still there. We learn in Better Call Saul though that he was released and went back to New Orleans.

(729) You can actually buy Breaking Bad cufflinks online.

(730) Jane Margolis has a 2005 Subaru Outback. We don't see her driving it though.

(731) You can buy quite an extensive range of Breaking Bad stickers.

(732) Giancarlo Esposito said he doesn't eat much fast food but he does like fried chicken. So perhaps he might pop into Los Pollos Hermanos if it was real.

(733) The desert landscapes that often feature in Breaking Bad symbolize the moral emptiness and isolation of Walter's new world.

(734) Lalo Salamanca is named after the composer Lalo Schifrin.

(735) The original plan for Better Call Saul was that Jimmy would become the Saul of Breaking Bad at the end

of season one. However, they discovered there was so much rich material to be mined from exploring Jimmy that most of the show took place before Breaking Bad and Jimmy's slide into Saul.

(736) Jonathan Banks was 75 by the time Better Call Saul ended and he'd shot his last scenes as Mike.

(737) Walter using Elliott and Gretchen as a means to leave Walt Jr and Holly a nest egg shows us that Walt has finally let go of his biggest weakness - his pride/ego. Walt Jr will never know that his father got him that money. He'll think it was Elliott and Gretchen.

(738) When they were shooting a desert sequence for Better Call Saul, the crew found a pregnant stray dog that was clearly not in great shape. Bob Odenkirk arranged for the dog to be cared for and given medical treatment and then made sure all the puppies found a loving home when they were born.

(739) Walt Jr's Dodge Challenger, and the fact he only had it for 15 hours, is inspired by the cult 1971 film Vanishing Point - in which a man named Kowalski, played by Barry Newman, is tasked with driving a 1970 Dodge Challenger from Colorado to San Francisco in record time.

(740) The Simpsons has made several comedic references to Breaking Bad.

(741) Javier Grajeda, who played Juan Bolsa in Breaking Bad, was roommates with Bryan Cranston in the 1980s. They were both in a show called Cover-Up.

(742) Hank references Terms of Endearment in Breaking

Bad. Terms of Endearment is a 1983 American comedy-drama film directed by James L. Brooks, starring Shirley MacLaine, Debra Winger, Jack Nicholson, Danny DeVito, Jeff Daniels, and John Lithgow. The film tells the story of a mother-daughter relationship that spans over several decades. We can probably presume that Marie made Hank sit through this film!

(743) Vince Gilligan said that Walter White's biggest superpower is his ability to lie constantly.

(744) Jesse is a hostage at the neo-Nazi compound in the back end of Breaking Bad and it is Todd who has to keep an eye on him. Jesse Plemons said in an interview that Todd probably thinks of Jesse as something akin to a pet dog!

(745) Bryan Cranston said he grew very fond of Albuquerque and now owns a house there. He said he loves the New Mexico food.

(746) Hank Shrader drives a Jeep Commander Sport.

(747) Laura Fraser said that she got the part of Lydia Rodarte-Quayle because she was living in New York at the time and heard they were casting for this part. She did two taped auditions and was then offered the part.

(748) Betsy Brandt is another cast member who said she assumed Breaking Bad was a comedy when she was auditioning during the casting.

(749) Vince Gilligan said he tried to make Walter likeable at the start of Breaking Bad so that his transformation into a criminal would be more startling.

(750) Most writers are unhappy when their dialogue is cut from an episode but Vince Gilligan said he never felt this way on Breaking Bad. He said he was always happy to cut a few lines because it made the show more cinematic.

(751) Heisenberg's sunglasses are Smith Optics Turnable sunglasses.

(752) Methamphetamine production involves a number of hazardous chemicals. Walter White is clearly wise to this because he insists on hazmat suits and gas masks.

(753) Vince Gilligan said that when the Breaking Bad spin-off show Better Call Saul was being planned his biggest fear was that it would turn out to be another AfterMASH. M*A*S*H was one of the most popular and beloved TV shows in history and so, when it ended in 1983, CBS were attracted to the concept of a spin-off show. The result was AfterMASH - the premise of which saw the characters Colonel Potter, Klinger and Father Mulcahy reunite to work at a veterans hospital in Missouri after the end of the Korean War. AfterMASH was later called one of the worst decisions of the century by Time Magazine and listed as the seventh worst TV show ever by TV Guide. It was cancelled nine episodes into its second season and has been almost completely forgotten today. There may even be fans of M*A*S*H who have no clue that AfterMASH exists out there in the lost etha of TV history.

(754) The character of Lalo, who was memorably played by Tony Dalton in Better Call Saul, was mentioned but unseen in Breaking Bad.

(755) Charles Baker was in his early 40s when playing Skinny Pete in the last season so he was considerably

older than the character he was playing.

(756) Laura Fraser said of her character Lydia Rodarte-Quayle - "Lydia vibrates at this high-pitched frequency, there is always nervous intensity."

(757) Jesse Pinkman's second car in Breaking Bad was a Toyota Tercel.

(758) Vince Gilligan said that Breaking Bad was sort of like Ikiru - only flipped on its head. Ikiru is a 1952 Japanese drama film by Akira Kurosawa about a man who gets cancer and decides to try and do something positive with what time he has left.

(759) Bryan Cranston was 52 years-old when Breaking Bad started.

(760) Bob Odenkirk felt the key to the character of Saul/Jimmy is that he is someone who has never quite grown up. Despite his age he remains a very immature and irresponsible person.

(761) Jesse Plemons said he had no idea Todd was going to be that evil when he signed on for Breaking Bad!

(762) After the plane crash, Walter White gives a rather rambling speech at school about how the plane crash could have been worse and everyone should be thankful it wasn't a bigger disaster. Some saw this as a sign that Walter is sociopathic and doesn't care about the crash. While there might be something in that it seems more likely that Walter was trying to mitigate his own sense of guilt for playing a part in the disaster.

(763) Walter White has a chemistry Ph.D. and

contributed to Nobel Prize-winning research. This might explain why Walt feels unappreciated in life. Despite all of his intelligence and science credentials he doesn't seem to have gotten on the fast track of life.

(764) Vince Gilligan said he is squemish when it comes to violence and blood and there were bits of Breaking Bad that he struggled to watch.

(765) You can go on a Breaking Bad tour in Albuquerque where a guide will show you the locations used for places like Los Pollos Hermanos, The Car Wash, Walt's House, Saul's Office, The Superlab, and so on. The tour seems to have very good reviews.

(766) Ed Begley Jr read for the part of Chuck McGill in Better Call Saul. In the end he was assigned the role of Clifford Main.

(767) In the Italian language version of Breaking Bad, the show is called Collateral Effects.

(768) In the episode Ozymandias, Hank tells Walt that he is the smartest man he has ever met but that Walt has failed to read what Jack Welker has already decided. This illustrates how Walt, despite his criminal activities, still doesn't really understand criminals and killers. Hank on the other hand, after years in law enforcement, can read criminals like Jack only too well.

(769) Giancarlo Esposito said he would love to play Hannibal Lecter. He said Anthony Hopkins told him he'd be good in the role too.

(770) It is often assumed that Walter White wanted Gale Boetticher dead because he deduced that once Gale knew

all the Blue Sky meth secrets Gus would have no need for Walter and replace him with Gale. Walter, according to this theory, feared for his life if Gale got really good at making Blue Sky meth. While there might be something in that it is also the case that Walter wanted Jesse back in the fold because he didn't want Jesse out there on the street as a rival making his own meth. He also didn't want Jesse pressing charges against Hank either. Another factor is that Walter clearly did not enjoy having a lab assistant who was more or less as clever as he was. That sort of thing is a dent to Walt's ego. He liked it much better when his cooking partner was Jesse - who he could control and manipulate.

(771) Breaking Bad has been parodied in shows like Saturday Night Live and Jimmy Kimmel Live.

(772) Jonathan Banks said that Mike's 'half-measures' speech was one of his favorite moments in the show because it was rare for the taciturn Mike to get a big monologue.

(773) Any color in meth is a sign of impurity so if Walter's meth really was that pure it shouldn't have any color.

(774) In the pilot, Skylar makes extra money be selling items on eBay. This was sort of forgotten after that but was referenced again much later.

(775) In the spin-off show Better Call Saul, Jimmy says that Kim has been 'sent to the cornfield' when she is forced to do tedious admin work. This is a reference to the Twilight Zone episode It's A Good Life. In this episode a town is held hostage by Anthony Fremont (Bill Mumy), a little boy with powerful psychic powers. Anthony has a penchant for sending people who have annoyed him out

to the cornfield after turning them into jack-in-the-boxes.

(776) The pink teddy bear that falls in Walter's pool also symbolizes the collateral damage caused by his criminal activities.

(777) Tony Dalton was given a lot of freedom to craft Lalo Salamanca in Better Call Saul. His approach was to make Lalo a more jovial and intelligent sort of man than the other Salamancas. Lalo is quite charming at times - although no less dangerous than his relatives.

(778) Before he appeared in Breaking Bad, Jesse Plemons was best known for his role as Landry Clarke in Friday Night Lights.

(779) You can buy 'bobblehead' figures of most of the characters from Breaking Bad.

(780) Giancarlo Esposito said he liked the fact that Breaking Bad was not a simplistic hero driven show. All the characters are human and have flaws.

(781) On Etsy, you can buy a Breaking Bad themed birthday card which features Jesse Pinkman saying - Yo, Happy Birthday Bitch!

(782) A lot of people have made Breaking Bad themed birthday cakes. They are of course usually finished with a generous sprinkle of blue rock candy on the top.

(783) Tuco Salamanca was the first person to sample Blue Sky meth.

(784) Vince Gilligan didn't want the character Lalo to be in Better Call Saul. He later said he was wrong about this

because Tony Dalton was so good.

(785) Daniel and Luis Moncada, who played the enforcers Leonel and Marco Salamanca, have tattoos on their eyelids from their gang days. That sounds incredibly painful!

(786) Walter White ends up earning tens of millions of dollars in Breaking Bad from making meth. Vince Gilligan has pointed out though that there is no way Walter could actually spend or invest this money without attracting the attention of the authorities. There is only a finite amount that can be laundered through a car wash.

(787) A subtext in Breaking Bad is the deconstruction of the American Dream. Walter's initial motivation to cook and sell methamphetamine is driven by his desire to leave a financial legacy for his family. However, as he becomes increasingly consumed by his criminal activities, the show examines how this pursuit of wealth and power ultimately destroys his relationships and leads to his downfall.

(788) Walter White's descent into the criminal underworld is driven by his addiction to power and success, showcasing the destructive nature of unchecked ambition.

(789) Jimmy's ramshackle yellow car at the start of Better Call Saul with the mismatched red door is very similar to Simon's car in the British comedy series The Inbetweeners. Was this an Easter egg? If it was no one from Better Call Saul has said so. It could just be a coincidence.

(790) When he was a jobbing young actor trying to pay the bills, Bryan Cranston was in a cheapjack science

fiction film called Dead Space. Oddly enough, in the film he plays a scientist with a cough!

(791) There is an interesting twist in Breaking Bad in that Gus Fring initially respects Walter and wants rid of his junkie assistant Jesse. In the end though Gus comes to trust Jesse more than he does Walter.

(792) RJ Mitte got less scenes as Walt Jr in later seasons because in real life he was now in his late teens and looking a bit too old to be that playing that character (who is obviously supposed to be younger as Breaking Bad doesn't take place over a long stretch of time).

(793) Lydia takes her tea with Stevia. Stevia is a sweetener and sugar substitute that comes from the leaves of the Stevia rebaudiana plant. It is much sweeter than sugar but has zero calories.

(794) Tortuga's explosive fate in the in desert is foreshadowed by his name. Tortuga is Spanish for tortoise.

(795) The car that Skylar buys Walt Jr in Salud is a Chrysler PT Cruiser. Walt Jr is clearly not terribly excited by this car.

(796) Giancarlo Esposito said that Box Cutter was his favorite episode.

(797) There is apparently a South Korean remake of Breaking Bad in the works.

(798) Tuco's name in Breaking Bad is inspired by Tuco Ramírez - the cunning Mexican bandit played by Eli Wallach in The Good, the Bad and the Ugly.

(799) Dead Freight has references to Once Upon a Time in the West and The Great Train Robbery.

(800) The average price of methamphetamine can range from $50 to $150 per gram. However, prices can be higher or lower depending on the availability and demand in a particular area.

(801) American Dad! has a Breaking Bad parody episode called Faking Bad.

(802) Breaking Bad has been compared to Shakespearean tragedy for its exploration of themes like power, morality, and hubris.

(803) Jesse says in the show that Walter White should not be underestimated and is really lucky. A scientist like Walter would probably say there is no such thing as luck.

(804) The translation of Juan Bolsa in English is Johnny Sack. Johnny Sack was a character in The Sopranos.

(805) In the second episode of season one, Walter says hydrofluoric acid will not dissolve polyethylene and tells Jesse to buy a polyethylene container. Plastics, generally made of long chains of carbon atoms, are relatively inert to weak acids like hydrofluoric acid. Hydrofluoric acid has a unique property in which it forms a protective layer of fluoride salts on the surface of certain materials, including some plastics, which can inhibit further reactions.

(806) There is a Better Call Saul episode where Gus says that he has seven restaurants. He has fourteen in Breaking Bad so Gus evidently doubled the size of his fast food empire in the years between each show.

(807) Aaron Paul, like Vince Gilligan, Dean Norris and Bryan Cranston, also had a connection with The X-Files. Aaron was in the episode Lord of the Flies.

(808) Saul Goodman was an important character for the writers on Breaking Bad because he could be used to deliver exposition and explain things but in an entertaining way that didn't feel clunky. Saul is the person who has to explain things like money laundering to Walter and Jesse and also the audience watching at home.

(809) You can see lots of weird imagery behind Gale Boetticher when he sings Major Tom (Coming Home) for the karaoke performance. This was put in by the Breaking Bad team. They cut in a load of clips from old television shows.

(810) The cabin that Walter hides out in as Mr Lambert is presumably near the border because Ed says it can pick up Québec television stations.

(811) Michael McKean played Chuck McGill in Better Call Saul. When he started work on Better Call Saul, Michael McKean was actually appearing in a play with Bryan Cranston. It is sometimes reported that it was Bryan who suggested Michael for the part.

(812) In the episode Rabid Dog, Hank seems to have a Breaking Bad DVD on his bookshelf!

(813) Bustle ranked Tuco Salamanca and Jack Welker as the two most evil characters in Breaking Bad.

(814) Francesca Liddy (played by Tina Parker) is Saul Goodman's long suffering secretary. In the prequel show

we see that Francesca was friendly and enthusiastic when first hired by Jimmy and Kim. However, by the time of Breaking Bad she is cynical and doesn't suffer fools gladly. Francesca is well aware that Saul is a crook and she has been a participant in this crookery herself. Francesca is now world weary and bitter. She is well aware that her association with Saul is probably not going to end very well for either of them.

(815) There was a special charity funeral for Walter White in Albuquerque when the show ended. The event was to raise money for the city's HealthCare for the Homeless organization.

(816) As part of his research and preparation for playing Walter White, Bryan Cranston spent some time with Michael Quinlan - the general chemistry lab coordinator at the University of Southern California.

(817) Sam Webb, who played Drew Sharp (the kid on the motorbike in Dead Freight), said the hardest thing about his part was falling over convincingly!

(818) The last car Jesse Pinkman has in the Breaking Bad universe is a 1988 Toyota Land Cruiser. This is the car Jesse has at the end of El Camino. It was obviously Ed Galbraith who supplied the vehicle.

(819) In the episode Box-Cutter, after their grisly clean up operation, Walter and Jesse are wearing Kenny Rogers t-shirts in the diner. These shirts were obviously the quickest things they (or perhaps Mike?) could buy.

(820) It is probably fair to say that, in terms of ratings and publicity, Breaking Bad was a bit overshadowed by AMC's other prestige show Mad Men in its early days.

(821) Gale Boetticher's surname was inspired by Budd Boetticher. Budd Boetticher was an American film director best known for low-budget Westerns starring Randolph Scott.

(822) Aaron Paul said in an interview that he felt Jesse's loyalty to Walter White was a consequence of Jesse's desperate search for a father figure and some sense of stability.

(823) As we have noted, Mike Ehrmantraut was invented to carry some plot intended for Saul Goodman when Bob Odenkirk became unavailable. Bob Odenkirk was booked to appear on How I Met Your Mother - so you have actually that show to thank for the invention of Mike Ehrmantraut.

(824) An alternative song they considered having Gale Boetticher sing in the karaoke clip was Orinoco Flow by Enya. This plan was abandoned because Enya wasn't interested and no permission or communication was forthcoming. It seems that Enya wasn't a Breaking Bad viewer.

(825) Bryan Cranston said he didn't do any method acting on Breaking Bad. Once shooting was wrapped for the day he would quickly shrug Walter White off and become Bryan Cranston again.

(826) Skylar drives a red Jeep Grand Wagoneer.

(827) You can buy a Breaking Bad Heisenberg Funko Pop.

(828) Laura Fraser said the first scene she shot in Breaking Bad was Lydia's meeting with Mike in the diner. Laura said she was very nervous - which actually helped

as Lydia is nervous too. Laura Fraser said that Jonathan Banks was very nice and gave her some pasta when the scene was over.

(829) Aaron Paul had a number of everyday jobs while he was trying to make it as an actor. At one point he was a delivery boy for Pizza Hut.

(830) Younger viewers may know Giancarlo Esposito best for his role as Moff Gideon in The Mandalorian.

(831) Aaron Paul unsuccessfully auditioned for a part in Malcom in the Middle - which of course featured his future Breaking Bad co-star Bryan Cranston. In case you were wondering, the part Aaron Paul auditioned for was Francis.

(832) The last ever role of Mark Margolis was, appropriately enough, in the television show Your Honor with Bryan Cranston.

(833) In the episode Phoenix, Walter was originally supposed to murder Jane by injection or other means but this was changed to him simply doing nothing while she slipped away. It was felt that at this still relatively early stage in the show it would have been too abrupt for Walter to kill someone in this fashion.

(834) Aaron Paul was already in his late twenties when Breaking Bad began but they gave him the part anyway because they liked his acting. The age difference between Aaron Paul and Jesse is more pronounced in the film El Camino - where Jesse is supposed to be in his mid-twenties but Aaron Paul was 40 in real life.

(835) Vince Gilligan thinks that Ozymandias is the best

episode of Breaking Bad.

(836) Gus Fring makes his first appearance in the episode Mandala.

(837) Vince Gilligan said that although he loves science he never took chemistry as a subject.

(838) It is actually Hank who, unwittingly, helped create Heisenberg because in the first episode he took Walter on a drive during a drugs bust and talked about how lucrative meth production could be for criminals. Hank obviously had no way way of knowing that Walter was going to start making meth himself!

(839) Bob Odenkirk said that listening to Robert Evans narrate his memoir influenced the way that Saul Goodman speaks. The charismatic film producer Robert Evans was the golden boy of Hollywood in the late sixties and seventies running Paramount Studio and producing classics like Rosemary's Baby, Chinatown, Harold and Maude, and The Godfather films.

(840) Vince Gilligan said he only thought Breaking Bad would last one season. He didn't think it would find an audience.

(841) According to Breaking Bad, Saul Goodman/Jimmy had three wives. Better Call Saul mentions that two marriages were dissolved before he married Kim Wexler.

(842) During the run of Breaking Bad, Bryan Cranston got a fan letter from no lesser figure than Sir Anthony Hopkins praising him for his performance as Walter White.

(843) When production began on the show money was tight. The set for Walter's house interior was constructed in a warehouse that had no electricity or hot water.

(844) Walt Jr was based on a student with cerebral palsy that Vince Gilligan knew at university.

(845) Marie Schrader's kleptomania is what could probably describe as an abandoned plot thread. It is established that Maria has a propensity to steal things but then this is sort of forgotten. I suppose you could say Marie and Hank had much bigger things to worry about in the end.

(846) The writers on Better Call Saul said that it was hard work at first because they knew absolutely nothing about the law and courts!

(847) The real location for the car wash that Walt and Skylar own in Breaking Bad is 9516 Snow Heights Cir. NE, Albuquerque, NM 87112.

(848) The name Ehrmantraut, as Better Call Saul reveals, is of German origin. It is an Americanized form of German Ehrmanntraut metronymic from an ancient Germanic female personal name composed of the elements irmin 'world all-encompassing' + trud 'strength'. Vince Gilligan had used this name in his previous work (like The X-Files). His inspiration for using this name is that he had friends named Ehrmantraut in Virginia.

(849) One of the clever things about Better Call Saul is that it isn't constricted by the conventions of a prequel. Prequels are quite common in film and television but they are not easy to do well and can come off as unnecessary. The brilliant thing about Better Call Saul is that it is not

only a prequel but also moves parallel to Breaking Bad and then beyond the base show into the future.

(850) Vince Gilligan said that the background of Gus Fring and what he really did in Chile was deliberately left a bit on the vague side because they thought the character would be more effective if the audience had to use their imagination and flesh out Gus Fring for themselves.

(851) RJ Mitte (jokingly) suggested a spin-off show where Walt Jr seeks revenge on Jesse Pinkman for helping his father become a criminal. Vince Gillgan said that while he'd love to work with Mitte again on something he has no interest in a Walt Jr spin-off show.

(852) Jonathan Banks said he thought it was right that Mike got killed because he was a villain. Although we like Mike for his deadpan wit and he has admirable qualities (like taking care of his family, loyalty, trying to see right by his men when it comes to money) the bottom line is that he is an enforcer and killer for a drug baron and many lives have doubtless been ruined by the drugs that Gus Fring supplies.

(853) Bryan Cranston said he usually tried to eat for real in scenes where Walt is having breakfast or meals to make it more realistic. Bryan said he hates it when you watch a TV show show and the actors are plainly just pushing food around their plate and not actually eating anything.

(854) We don't learn anything about Ed Galbraith's background. All we know is that, for the right price, he can give you a new identity and make you disappear.

(855) The series finale is called Filena. Fe Li Na, on the

periodic table, translates to iron, lithium, and sodium. You can further translate this into Blood, Meth, Tears.

(856) The song Baby Blue by Badfinger was used in the last ever scene in Breaking Bad. This led to online streams of the song increasing by 9000%.

(857) Walter and Walt Jr are not very impressed in Pilot when Skylar serves them vegetarian bacon for breakfast. Vegetarian products like this are primarily made from soy. The vegan and vegetarian plant based foods you can buy now are very good once you get used to them.

(858) Marie drives a Volkswagon Beetle in Breaking Bad.

(859) Other video games we see Jesse playing in the show are Sonic & SEGA All-Stars Racing and Sonic the Hedgehog.

(860) Michael Bowen, who played the neo-Nazi gang member Jack, is half-Jewish. Michael said that he finds it a bit weird that people sometimes think he's like Jack in real life.

He said he was in a store once and someone asked him for meth!

(861) When the show was preparing to launch, AMC did get some letters of complaint from people worried that the show might make meth and crime seem appealing. Those fears were assuaged though by the actual show - which makes neither meth nor crime seem like much fun at all.

(862) The first Breaking Bad episode went out the same night as the NFC championship game. The game went

into overtime - which basically meant that hardly anyone was watching Breaking Bad when it started!

(863) Vince Gilligan said the early network rejections for Breaking Bad didn't especially surprise him because he knew that a show about meth criminals wasn't going to be an easy sell.

(864) In real life, meth labs do not require a huge amount of equipment so meth production can sometimes be carried out in fairly small spaces.

(865) Michael Slovis, who was the director of photography on Breaking Bad from season two, said he and Vince Gilligan wanted to shoot the show in widescreen but were not given permission to do this.

(866) Saul Goodman ending up working in a mall under an assumed identity is truly like hell for the character. Jimmy always craved the limelight, fame, and wealth. He always wanted to be at the heart of the action. Having to live this mundane dull life as Gene and basically keep his head down and fade into the background is definitely his worst nightmare.

(867) It is probably safe to presume that Ed Galbraith launders some (but surely not all) of his ill gotten gains through his vacuum store.

(868) Vince Gilligan and Peter Gould said they gravitated towards Saul Goodman for the spin-off because they thought it would be interesting to see how this man ended up as a sleazy corrupt lawyer who fronts for drug dealers.

(869) Jonathan Banks said he didn't find it a huge stretch to transition to playing Mike in Better Call Saul. The

character was more or less the same in both shows.

(870) Aaron Paul said it was his idea for Jesse to shave his hair off in the show - or most of it anyway.

(871) In the scene where Saul accuses the DEA of harassing Mike, Hank asks Saul where he got his law degree from. We see that Saul is irritated by this question and he doesn't answer. In the spin-off show we see that Saul got his law degree by correspondence course while working in a mail room.

(872) Jesse has a 'skeleton' grenade t-shirt in Breaking Bad later on. This t-shirt was apparently made by a snowboarding company.

(873) Vince Gilligan said that one of Walter White's biggest problem and weaknesses was that he felt sorry for himself too much and had come to see himself as a victim who needed to somehow get revenge on the world.

(874) Lydia, despite her nervous and timid exterior, is one of the most ruthless characters in Breaking Bad. She will sanction the death of virtually anyone to protect her status and freedom. The only person Lydia cares about is her daughter.

(875) We see a scene in Breaking Bad where Hector is watching Bridge on the River Kwai in the old folks home. Bridge on the River Kwai is a 1957 film directed by David Lean and based on the novel of the same name by Pierre Boulle. The film follows a group of British prisoners of war in a Japanese prison camp during World War II who are forced to build a railway bridge over the River Kwai.

(876) The website that Hank is bidding for minerals on in

Breaking Bad is fictional. You obviously can bid for minerals online though with real websites.

(877) Breaking Bad was initially developed for the FX channel. However, in the end they only had room for one new show and chose to go with a Courtney Cox series called Dirt (which was about a tabloid magazine). Dirt ended after only two seasons and didn't really catch on. It was presumably the star power of Courtney Cox (who was coming off the back of Friends at the time) which made FX choose Dirt over Breaking Bad. They obviously had no way of knowing that Breaking Bad would become this classic beloved show.

(878) The casting director on Breaking Bad was Sharon Bialy. Sharon actually had the idea of casting Bryan Cranston even before she learned that Vince Gilligan wanted him too.

(879) In an interview after the last episode of Breaking Bad, Vince Gilligan suggested that Jesse would probably be arrested quite quickly because his prints would have been all over Jack's hideout. This obviously didn't turn out to be the case though in El Camino.

(880) In 2022 it was reported that Breaking Bad, despite ending several years ago, was still in the top ten of the most pirated television shows that year. Pirated obviously means shows watched through torrents or illegal streams.

(881) Aaron Paul said that the appearances by Jesse and Walter in Better Call Saul had to be 'organic'. They couldn't just be shoehorned in for the sake of it.

(882) In the episode Felina, Walter creates a booby trap with a M60 machine gun. Vince Gilligan appeared on the

show Mythbusters when they tested this scene for real to see if it was plausible. It turned out that it worked in real life so Walter's booby trap really was realistic.

(883) Oliver Stone, for reasons best known to himself, said in the media that Walter's machine gun booby trap in the last episode was silly and laughable. He obviously didn't watch Mythbusters!

(884) We see in Breaking Bad that Hank has some Cuban cigars which are not strictly legal. Due to trade restrictions, Cuban cigars are not widely available in the United States, making them a sought-after luxury item for cigar enthusiasts. Being in the DEA obviously has a few perks.

(885) Vince Gilligan said in a Reddit AMA that the most important thing in television drama is to have the characters behaving in what seems like a believable and human way to what is happening. If you can't relate to the characters then you can't invest in the show.

(886) Dean Norris said it was fun to play the 'macho swagger' Hank we see at the start of Breaking Bad. Hank transforms into a more troubled, depressed, and vulnerable character in subsequent seasons.

(887) As the spin-off Better Call Saul drew to an end, Giancarlo Esposito told the media he'd be happy to do a spin-off show about Gus Fring. One could venture though that this ship has probably sailed (there can't be THAT much more to mine from Gus after BB & BCS and Esposito is probably getting a bit old now to play the part) - unless one did a show about Gus as a young man in Chile and a younger actor played the character.

(888) Vince Gilligan said that Walter White was his own worst enemy because of ego and pride and tendency to see himself as a victim. Vince said that Walter should have simply swallowed his pride and taken the 'lifeline' offered to him by Elliott and Gretchen early on.

(889) Bryan Cranston said his favorite line in Breaking Bad was when he confronted Hank in Blood Money and Walter tells him to 'tread lightly' because Hank doesn't really know him at all.

(890) The craziest Breaking Bad fan theory is that Mike Ehrmantraut is really Jesse Pinkman from the future and has come back to save himself!

(891) Mark Margolis said that playing Hector Salamanca was a fun challenge because he had to act through facial expressions.

(892) It is made clear in Breaking Bad that Saul is aware of Gus but we never see them meet. However, we do see them meet in Better Call Saul

(893) Walter uses a pipe bomb in his quest to kill Gus Fring. A pipe bomb is an improvised explosive device made from a metal pipe filled with explosive material. It is typically ignited by a fuse or trigger mechanism.

(894) Ed Galbraith's clients go into a 'safe house' beneath his vacuum store while preparations for their departure are made. A flashback in Better Call Saul shows us Saul and Walter sleeping down there while waiting for Ed to arrange their departures.

(896) An Erlenmeyer flask is a type of laboratory flask that has a flat bottom, a conical shape, and a narrow neck.

It is commonly used for titrations, heating liquids, and mixing chemicals. The conical shape allows for easy swirling of liquids without the risk of spilling. Erlenmeyer flasks are made from borosilicate glass, which is resistant to heat and chemical reactions. They are named after the German chemist Emil Erlenmeyer, who first designed them in the 19th century.

(897) In 2024 it was reported that the Mexican armed forces had 'busted' a meth superlab which had 4.13 metric tons (91,073 lb) of meth and 1.27 tons of precursor chemicals used to make the synthetic drug. Photographs from the bust showed it was a considerably more ramshackle and unhygienic operation than that of Gus Fring.

(898) Schraderbräu, the real beer that Dean Norris launched, seems to have pretty decent reviews online.

(899) A No-Rough-Stuff-Type Deal is a quote from the film Fargo. Fargo is a 1996 crime film directed by Joel and Ethan Coen.

(900) Blue Sky is the name of a real soda company in New Mexico.

(901) The train heist in Dead Freight was shot at a location off US-285 & Spur Ranch Rd.

(902) Saul Goodman refers to Ed Galbraith as 'the disappearer'. This is a very accurate term because Galbraith literally can make a person vanish without trace.

(903) Marius Stan, who played Walt's car wash boss Bogdan Wolynetz, actually has a PhD in chemistry in real

life. He's a real scientist.

(904) Walter White was originally going to be a younger character but it was decided that the show would work better if Walt was older. The idea is that Walt is having, to put it mildly, a life crisis. Not just a mid-life crisis but a LIFE crisis.

(905) The episode title Negro y Azul means black and blue in Spanish.

(906) The RV used by Walt and Jesse was a 1986 Fleetwood Bounder.

(907) Breaking Bad explores the consequences of one's actions and decisions - illustrating how they can have far-reaching effects on oneself and others. Walter kids himself that he is helping his family but in reality he makes life more difficult for them. Having said that though, Walt Jr should have a comfortable future thanks to the money Walter gave Elliott and Gretchen to give him!

(908) Samuel L. Jackson said he wanted to make a cameo in Breaking Bad but this obviously never happened.

(909) Vince Gilligan said that he originally planned to kill Hank at the end of the first season. He felt he needed a big dramatic death to hook viewers. As with other early planned deaths, the writer's strike made him reflect and change his plans.

(910) When he finished on Breaking Bad, Dean Norris took a number of things as momentoes. They included a DEA bomber jacket a prop of the axe which the crazy cousins tried to kill Hank with.

(911) RJ Mitte said he took home Walt Jr's crutches when the show ended.

(912) Albuquerque is situated along the Rio Grande river and is surrounded by the Sandia Mountains.

(913) In the episode 4 Days Out, Jesse asks Walt if he's building a robot. This line was suggested by the 1st AC, Nick Shuster. Vince Gillgan said it was one of his favorite moments in the show.

(914) Walter White adopts his goatee for good in ABQ.

(915) Winters in Albuquerque are mild with temperatures averaging in the 40s and 50s. Snowfall is rare in the city, but it does occasionally occur in the surrounding mountains.

(916) In the episode Full Measure, Mike rescues warehouse workers from cartel goons. The gun Mike uses in this sequence is a Heckler & Koch Mark 23. The gun is fitted with a silencer.

(917) Walter acquires a M60 machine gun in the last season. The M60 is a belt-fed general-purpose machine gun first adopted by the US military in 1957.

(918) In the film El Camino we see that Jesse can't actually remember the precise vacuum related question needed for Ed Galbraith's services. You can't blame him really. It is definitely something you'd need to write down on a piece of paper!

(919) Treatment for methamphetamine addiction typically involves a combination of therapy, counseling, and support groups, as well as medications to manage

withdrawal symptoms and cravings.

(920) Krysten Ritter was pregnant when she did her cameo in El Camino. They had to hide this.

(921) The FPS game RAGE had not actually come out when Jesse plays it in Breaking Bad. The production was given a special early version.

(922) Max Arciniega, Gus Fring's late business partner, is named after the actor who plays Krazy-8.

(923) The episode Salud suggests that it takes several hours for Jesse to produce a batch of Blue Sky meth.

(924) Salud means 'health' in Spanish.

(925) Walter White's father died when Walter was still a child. Walter tells Walt Jr that it was because of Huntington's disease. Huntington's disease is a progressive neurological disorder.

(926) Some of the stores in Albuquerque sell Blue Sky Breaking Bad bath salts.

(927) Bob Odenkirk said that on the last season of Breaking Bad he only read Saul Goodman's lines in the script so that he could watch it at home with no idea of what was going to happen to Walter and Jesse.

(928) Bryan Cranston did an interview in 2024 where he suggested that, with the end of Better Call Saul, it was time to gracefully end the Breaking Bad universe rather than try to keep the 'franchise' going with more prequels or spin-offs.

(929) Vince Gilligan said he doesn't mind if people have a preference between Breaking Bad and Better Call Saul. He is just happy that both shows turned out to be good.

(930) Jane Margolis has a line about 'throwing up in her mouth' when Jesse says something romantic. This rather anticipates her fate.

(931) After his stint on Breaking Bad, Dean Norris had a main role in the small screen adaptation of Stephen King's Under the Dome. The television version of Under the Dome was abysmal and Dean made no secret of being relieved (telling social media he was off to Disneyworld) when it was cancelled. As he noted though a lot more people watched Under the Dome than Breaking Bad because it was on CBS!

(932) Dr Donna Nelson, a chemistry professor from the University of Oklahoma, served as a science consultant on Breaking Bad.

(933) In 2014, Breaking Bad action figures were pulled from Toys R Us after a protest campaign in Florida which argued that meth dealers (even fictional ones it seems) should not become toys. The fact that adult Breaking Bad fans and toy collectors were the real market for these figures seemed to elude the protesters.

(934) Dave Porter composed the music for Breaking Bad, Better Call Saul, and El Camino. Other shows he worked on include Preacher and The Blacklist.

(935) Aaron Paul said he has never had any formal acting training.

(936) The word "madrigal" is derived from the Italian

word "madrigale," which means simple song or pastoral song.

(937) Vince Gilligan said that an early plan for season five was that Jesse would be arrested and in a prison bus and Jack's gang would attack the bus to kill Jesse but then Walter would use his newly aquired machine gun to save Jesse. In the end they decided this would be too silly and depict Walter White as Rambo!

(938) Vince Gilligan said another ending they discussed was having Walter break into jail with the machine gun to rescue Jesse. As with the prison bus idea they decided this was too silly and unrealistic to go ahead with.

(939) The vast majority of deaths in Breaking Bad came as a result of guns.

(940) Saul Goodman says in Breaking Bad that he has bad knees. This is explained by Better Call Saul - where we see he was a con artist called Slippin' Jimmy on the ice glazed streets of Chicago.

(941) A study by the National Institute on Drug Abuse in 2021 found that methamphetamine deaths in America had tripled in the previous five years.

(942) Breaking Bad is interesting in the way it shows us how people juggle different identities and sides of themselves. We all do this to some extent - though obviously not in the criminal and fictional way depicted in Breaking Bad! Jimmy McGill creates the crude persona of Saul Goodman to make himself rich, plain old nerdy Walter White becomes the dangerous Heisenberg, Gus Fring juggles his role as a placid and friendly fast food boss with that of a ruthless drug baron, Ed Galbraith is a

kind old vacuum store owner but secretly offers a service hiding criminals and killers, Mike is a loving grandfather but also a deadly assassin/enforcer for a drug kingpin, Jesse is playing the role of a street hood/addict when in reality he comes from a fairly well to do family, Hank takes the role of the tough fearless jokester when in reality he's more vulnerable and serious than anyone suspects, Walt Jr takes to calling himself Flynn. And so on.

(943) Walter White lives on Negra Arroyo Lane at the start of the show. This is obviously not the real name of the street used. Negra Arroyo loosely translates to 'black water' in Spanish.

(944) Bob Odenkirk said it was his idea to give Saul Goodman a bit of a mullet hairstyle at the back.

(945) In the pizza scene, Walter says he has dipping sticks too. Dipping sticks is another name for breadsticks.

(946) One of the last things Jesse does in El Camino is give Ed a letter to post to Brock. Ed is not a man who expresses any emotion but we plainly see he is touched by the letter.

(947) Game of Thrones author George R.R. Martin said that Heisenberg was a 'bigger monster' than any of the villains in his books.

(948) In the first episode of Better Call Saul, Jimmy parks his battered Suzuki Esteem next to a snazzy Cadillac DeVille. Saul Goodman (Jimmy) drives a Cadillac DeVille in Breaking Bad so it must have been the parking lot which gave him the idea to buy one if he ever got wealthier.

(949) Loyola's Restaurant is a place where Mike likes to eat in Breaking Bad. This is the restaurant where Jimmy meets the Kettlemans in Better Call Saul. Loyola's Family Restaurant is a real place in New Mexico where you can go to eat.

(950) Walt's pride in his meth is a tragic commentary on the fact that he could have been a famous scientist but is now reduced to being a criminal chemist who tries to make the most pure meth he can. It's all he has left.

(951) In the scene where Mike is at Loyola's Restaurant with Jesse, Mike is eating meatloaf and corn on the cob. He seems to have some gravy and potatoes too.

(952) Vince Gilligan said that they went out of their way to make a life of crime seem laborious, unpleasant, and a constant headache in Breaking Bad. While we wouldn't mind instant wealth we definitely wouldn't to go through what Walt and Jesse do to get that wealth.

(953) There was a real life case of (highly dangerous) red meth being sold on the streets in New Mexico. The dealers were clearly trying to make their 'product' distinctive.

(954) There is a possible goof in the episode ABQ. Mike Ehrmantraut wears gloves to clean up Jesse's apartment after Jane's death but he isn't wearing gloves when he opens the door before going in the house.

(955) Breaking Bad had 62 episodes. No. 62 on the periodic table is Samarium - which is used in the treatment of cancer.

(956) The pesky fly in the episode Fly was seen by many

(including Vince Gilligan) to represent Walter's conscience and guilt. The fly keeps nagging him and won't go away. We see Walter struggling to sleep at home in this episode too because of a fly. Guilt and regret in strong doses can cause sleepless nights.

(957) In the episode Live Free or Die, Mike says the police have a Halon system to save evidence in the event of a fire. Halon refers to a class of chemicals that used to be commonly used as fire extinguishing agents due to their effectiveness in suppressing fires. Halon has been largely phased out due to its harmful environmental impact.

(958) Jesse Plemons (who played Todd), has a definite resemblance to Matt Damon. After appearing in Breaking Bad he was nicknamed Meth Damon by fans.

(959) Norbert Weisser, who played the Madrigal executive Peter Schuler in Breaking Bad and Better Call Saul, is a German born actor who has been based in the United States for many years. He has been in everything from ER to The Rocketeer to Knight Rider. Trivia - Norbert Weisser played a Norwegian in John Carpenter's The Thing.

(960) You can buy blue-meth doughnuts in Albuquerque. The 'meth' is obviously candy and sugar and not real meth!

(961) Norbert Weisser was the voice of Adolf Hitler in the video game Wolfenstein II: The New Colossus.

(962) Saul suggests to Walt in Breaking Bad that he might send Hank 'on a trip to Belize' like he had done to Mike. Belize is a small country located in Central America, bordered by Mexico to the north, Guatemala to the west

and south, and the Caribbean Sea to the east. Belize became independent from Britain in 1981. The Belize tourist board actually used Saul's Breaking Bad quote in their marketing!

(963) Madrigal executive Peter Schuler commits suicide with an Automated External Defibrillator (AED). AEDs are portable devices used to treat sudden cardiac arrest by delivering an electric shock to the heart to restore its normal rhythm. AEDs are designed to be user-friendly and can be used by people with minimal training.

(964) Vince Gilligan said that Gus Fring's desire to get revenge for Max was his Achilles Heel. It was the one thing which made him do things which were not always cautious or logical.

(965) In season five, Walter and Jesse cook meth in a house that is temporarily empty while fumigation takes place. Vince Gilligan said that he highly doubts you could get away with this in real life!

(966) We see Hank eating Boulder Canyon chips at home in Breaking Bad. Boulder Canyon chips are gourmet kettle-cooked potato chips known for their crunchy texture and bold flavors. Hank is eating the sea salt and cracked pepper ones.

(967) Bryan Cranston's real life wife and daughter have little bit part cameos in the episode No Mas.

(968) In the early treatment for Breaking Bad, Hank's original surname was Weld.

(969) You can buy a lot of Breaking Bad themed trucker caps online.

(970) If you watched the whole of Breaking Bad with no breaks it would take you around 60 hours.

(971) Walter's pork pie hat in Breaking Bad is similar to the one worn by Detective Popeye Doyle (Gene Hackman) in The French Connection. This is a film that Hank references in season four. Doyle is trying to catch a drug smuggler named Charnier.

(972) Breaking Bad cost about $3 million an episode to make. This was quite a big budget for a cable show.

(973) Thanks to Netflix exposure and online word of mouth, Breaking Bad had audiences of ten million at the end. In its early says though only a few million watched the show.

(974) Hank is a fan of the film Heat. Heat is a crime thriller film directed by Michael Mann and released in 1995. The film stars Al Pacino and Robert De Niro as a detective and a career criminal who play cat and mouse. You could say that Hank is Pacino and Walt is De Niro!

(975) Laura Fraser, who played Lydia Rodarte-Quayle, is only 5'1 tall in real life.

(976) Walt and Jesse are held captive by the crazy meth kingpin Tuco early in Breaking Bad. Walter can't tell his family what really happened so he pretends he went into a fugue state and can't remember anything. During a fugue state, a person may temporarily lose their sense of personal identity and may wander aimlessly while unable to remember who they are or how they got there.

(977) Bryan Cranston was paid $225,000 per episode in the last season of Breaking Bad.

(978) Aaron Paul was paid $150,000 per episode in the last season of Breaking Bad.

(979) Warren Buffett was a big Breaking Bad fan and called Walter White a great businessman. Warren Buffett is an American investor, business tycoon, and philanthropist who is considered one of the most successful investors in the world.

(980) Dean Norris said he heard that Tom Hanks and Oprah Winfrey took Breaking Bad DVDs with them to watch when they went on a swanky yacht vacation!

(981) When the last episode of Breaking Bad went out, a large number of celebrities 'live' tweeted about the show on social media and said how much they had enjoyed it. They included Ellen DeGeneres, Michael Moore, Kevin Smith, Paul Feig, Ewan McGregor, Don Cheadle, Joyce Carol Oates, Mindy Kaling, Kristen Bell, Michael B. Jordan, Ed Sheerhan, Rosie O'Donnell, Conan O'Brien, and many others.

(982) Danny Trejo has a fairly brief role in Breaking Bad as Tortuga - the cartel runner who meets a gruesome end. Trejo said he quite enjoyed seeing a prop of his head in the show in that explosive desert scene.

(983) Walt Jr's best friend is Louis Corbett. This part was originally played by Kyle Swimmer but then recast with Caleb Jones taking over. The version of Louis played by Jones was nicer and less grungy in appearance than the one that Swimmer played. It seems they decided to something of an alteration with this character.

(984) Jesse is taken to Mexico in Breaking Bad to show the cartel how to make Blue Sky meth. This sort of thing

has happened in real life. A criminal gang in the United States who made and supplied ecstasy (MDMA) once struck a lucrative deal with a Mexican cartel to go Mexico and teach the cartel their MDMA secrets and methods. However, the Americans aborted the plan when they deduced that the cartel planned to kill them once they'd got the information they needed.

(985) In the episode Problem Dog, Walter takes Walt Jr's car out for a spin and skids it around. The location for this scene is the Isleta Amphitheatre Parking Lot located at 5601 University Blvd. The location was right next to where the real DEA office was in Albuquerque.

(986) In the spin-off show Better Call Saul, the flash forward has the fugitive Jimmy living under an assumed identity in Omaha and working in a mall. However, Jimmy is recognized by a cab driver named Jeff who lived in Albuquerque and is well aware that Gene is Saul Goodman. Jeff intends to use this to his advantage and blackmail Jimmy. Don Harvey played Jeff when he was introduced but later - to the confusion of many viewers - Jeff is played by Pat Healy. The reason why this happened is that Don Harvey was signed up to another show and couldn't come back to Better Call Saul. So they had to recast the part. Harvey's version of Jeff was more sinister and menacing whereas Healy gave us a more comedic and less threatening version of Jeff.

(987) There are 27 deaths in season three of Breaking Bad.

(988) In the flashback which shows us the murder of Max by Don Eladio Vuente's pool, Hector clearly aims what can be construed as homophobic comments at Gus.

(989) Skinny Pete plays the piano in Hazard Pay. That was really Charles Baker (the actor who played Pete) playing too. He is playing Solfeggietto by Bach.

(990) The little girl who played Lydia's daughter in Breaking Bad was actually the same age with the exact same birthday as Laura Fraser's real life daughter.

(991) A big part of Walter White's character is that he has no empathy for anyone outside of his family - save for Jesse (whom Walt has some fluctuating paternal instincts towards). You get the impression Walter would pull the plug on the entire world to preserve his family life.

(992) The flashback which shows the murder of Gus Fring's associate Max takes place in 1989.

(993) Crazy Handful of Nothing is a quote from the film Cool Hand Luke. Cool Hand Luke is a 1967 film directed by Stuart Rosenberg and starring Paul Newman as the titular character, Luke Jackson. Luke is a charismatic and rebellious prisoner who refuses to conform to the strict rules and authority of the chain gang where he is incarcerated.

(994) The spin-off show Better Call Saul shows us how Jimmy/Saul and Mike Ehrmantraut first met. Mike was the booth attendant at the courthouse parking lot and wouldn't let Jimmy go through because he didn't have enough stickers. It is classic Mike Ehrmantraut that he is taking his role as a parking booth attendant very seriously - to the point of being pedantic!

(995) Another ringtone Todd has in Breaking Bad is She Blinded Me With Science. She Blinded Me With Science is a song by English musician Thomas Dolby, released in

1982.

(996) The Ranker website has Walter White ranked as the greatest ever television character. Michael Scott (from The Office) and Tony Soprano were the closest competitors.

(997) We see Jesse make huevos rancheros for Jane's breakfast in Breaking Bad. Huevos rancheros is a traditional Mexican breakfast dish consisting of fried eggs served on top of corn tortillas, topped with salsa, avocado, and sometimes beans or cheese. It is typically served with a side of refried beans and rice.

(998) The superheroes that Jesse tells Jane he invented as a teenager are named Kanga-Man, Rewindo, and Hover.

(999) Breaking Bad has a stellar audience rating of 97% on Rotten Tomatoes.

(1000) Felina, the title of the last ever episode, is an anagram for Finale.

www.ingramcontent.com/pod-product-compliance
Lightning Source LLC
Chambersburg PA
CBHW020545160726
47991CB00002B/588